Work that Matters

BRIDGING THE DIVIDE
BETWEEN WORK AND WORSHIP

KEVIN BROWN • MICHAEL WIESE

Work that Matters: Bridging the Divide between Work and Worship

ALDERSGATE PRESS

THE PUBLICATIONS ARM OF

WESLEYAN HOLINESS CONSORTIUM

HolinessAndUnity.org

In Collaboration with
EMETH PRESS
www.emethpress.com
Lexington, Kentucky

Library of Congress Cataloging-in-Publication Data

Brown, Kevin.
 Work that matters : bridging the divide between work and worship /
Kevin Brown, Michael Wiese.
      pages cm
 Includes bibliographical references and index.
 ISBN 978-1-60947-067-8 (alk. paper)
 1. Work--Religious aspects--Christianity. 2. Worship. I. Wiese, Michael. II.
Title.
 BT738.5.B75 2013
 248.8'8--dc23
                        2013039172

Contents

Introduction

Does your life story sometimes feel like you are living two or more different scripts? As a Christian, you know that God is the author of your story. But when you go to work the script seems to change. Maybe you simply accept it. Or, knowing this is not right, you strive to find ways to bring your two worlds—your spiritual life and your work life—in harmony. Yet there is tension. You are divided between *work* and *worship*.

Is it possible to have a life that embraces work *as* worship, to live in a way that brings unity to life? This book is for those who want our lives to be whole. Do you want the script of your life to consistently stand for Christ? If so, consider the following story.

Stick to the Script!

The year 1909 provided what continues to be one of the more interesting sports stories of all time. It involves a boxing match between middle-weight champion Stanley Ketchel and an imposing African-American boxer named Jack Johnson. Few white fighters would risk taking on Johnson. He was brash, wore fancy suits, drove fast cars, and dated white women. In other words, he didn't fit the white-black race conventions of early twentieth-century America—but he could fight. When promoters put enough money on the table to defeat the Goliath-like Johnson, the search was on for what would later be referred to as the "great white hope."

Ketchel was one fighter up to the challenge. Unfortunately, as skilled as he was (he had earned the nickname "The Michigan Assassin"), he was severely undersized and hopelessly underweight compared to his opponent. He had no chance of defeating Johnson and both men knew it. Interestingly, Ketchel and Johnson were friends and often could be found gambling, drinking, and even attending brothels together. Ever mindful of making an extra buck, they agreed to fight, but with certain conditions. The match would be twenty rounds. The longer the match, the more it would create additional revenue in the theaters. Thus, boxing lore has it that Ketchel and Johnson made an agreement before the fight. Johnson would not knock out Ketchel as long as he agreed not to try winning the match. To achieve this, the fighters would fall into a type of a dance. The strategy was in place—all they had to do was "stick to the script."

As expected, the outdoor stadium was filled to capacity. The two fighters jabbed, picked, wrestled, and danced from the opening bell. While punches were thrown and blows were landed, the two fighters stayed within their pre-determined pact. However, something happened in the twelfth round that would change this arrangement altogether. Ketchel, in a sudden moment, decided to stray from the script and do the unthinkable: he decided to try to knock Johnson out. Detecting an opening, he launched his right arm and landed a thunderous blow on Johnson's face. Johnson, stunned, hit the mat. Almost immediately a sea of white spectators exploded out of their seats in jubilation. The mighty Jack Johnson had fallen! The sports world was set right. The great white hope had been discovered.

That is, there was hope until Johnson got up. Once up, he was no longer dancing. Ketchel had abandoned the script, so Johnson would too. The duration of the bout after the angered fighter arose lasted less than five seconds. Johnson delivered two devastating blows that sent an unconscious Ketchel flailing to the mat. It was later discovered that one of these punches was so severe that Ketchel's teeth were embedded in Johnson's glove. The victor calmly made his way to the ropes and simply stared at Ketchel's motionless body. In Ken Burn's epic documentary of Jack Johnson titled *Unforgivable Blackness*, one sports commentator appropriately describes Ketchel's error: "The moral of the story…follow the script."

Divided Hearts

Stanley Ketchel desired to serve two masters, to be both victorious and faithful. In the heat of the moment, the real agenda came out and he discovered what he was really living for…and it got him knocked him out. While not endorsing the deception of the plan, the Ketchel-Johnson match is a fitting metaphor for a larger, more human, story.

It is the sad tale of trying to live under different identities, having a divided heart, harboring multiple—and often contradictory—aims. As a Christian, do you find yourself changing

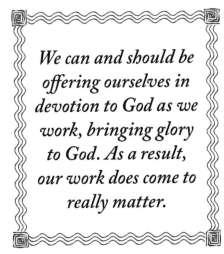

We can and should be offering ourselves in devotion to God as we work, bringing glory to God. As a result, our work does come to really matter.

your life script as you transition from your worship life on Sunday to your work life on Monday? Are you like Ketchel? Or is it your desire to "stick to the script" of God's work in your life?

When at work, do you feel the tension of a divided heart? Is there a possibility of competing agendas? Elijah once scolded the prophets of Baal for trying to harbor competing identities: "How long will you go limping with two different opinions? If the Lord is God, follow him; but if Baal, then follow him" (1 Kings 18:21). When people limp, something is wrong. They are not walking correctly. They are wavering between two beliefs, identities, and worldviews, contrasting postures that cannot occupy the same space.

This book is a warning against harboring competing identities. Our purpose is to call Christians to see work as an act of worship. As we work we can be offering ourselves in devotion to God and our efforts can bring glory to God. As a result, our work does come to matter.

Specifically, we will explore what it means to be *a person of faith in a working world*. On the surface, there may seem to be little conflict between being a person of faith in Jesus Christ and a participant in the working world. Countless nurses, teachers, construction workers, architects, writers, plumbers, government agents, and musicians identify themselves as Christians. While there is nothing odd about Christians finding themselves in various places of employment, there is something very wrong with Christians having a *split identity* while on the job. Therefore, we will look carefully at what it means to be persons of faith in our various workplaces. Like Ketchel, we may be surprised how a divided heart knocks out integrity and witness potential.

How should a Christian relate *work* and *worship*? In chapter one, we will explore the current work-worship divide. The good news is that there is a way that we can view our work as an act of faith. Then we will consider a faithful way of viewing work that brings our worship and work into harmony. The goal is to live a whole and holy life for God's glory.

Reflect for Yourself or for Discussion with Others

1. Do you feel divided between your life at work and your commitment to Christ?

2. As you go to work, are your thoughts on using the work for God's glory or do you just want to survive the day so that you can get back to your "real life" and "real self?"

3. As you work, do you consider your activity an act of worship? Do you think it is possible to do so?

CHAPTER 1

The Work-Worship Divide

Holiness and wholeness are the full,
undivided presence of God.

Seeking to be a follower of Christ, our desire should be
to live a transformed life through the redeeming work
of God. If holiness is our goal, is it appropriate to live a
divided life? There must be wholeness and integrity in our
lives both in and out of our work settings. Being "undivided" should be a central goal for the Christian. The script of
our lives should speak of the presence of God regardless of
our setting, church, home, work or play.

In this chapter, we will consider the undivided life and
then some of the common work-worship divides that frag-
ment our living and undermine our ability to live in wholeness. Before proceeding, we need a common understanding
of terms.

Work: activities that we engage in to sustain our physical and financial lives.

Worship: spiritual activities and expressions, enabled by the Holy Spirit, that we engage in to honor God, express our love to God, and live in God's presence.

Holiness: Living a life fully dedicated to Christ, with the intention of letting the example of Jesus shape our thoughts, words, and deeds.

Wholeness: Consistent with holiness, wholeness is to live in integrity, without divides between who we are in one setting in contrast to who we are in another. Wholeness is arranging, managing, and navigating our lives in a unified manner.

Simply put, we want to live a life that reflects the work of Jesus Christ and one that consistently displays the presence of God shaping us and using us for His purposes. If a majority of our waking hours are devoted to some form of work, should we not be intentional about finding ways to redeem that time as an expression of honor, love and commitment to God? As Martin Luther taught us centuries ago, we are all in ministry and our vocation (our work) is part of our ministry. Our work is our "calling." As we work, is God inviting us to worship? Our work matters. As Christians, instead of being divided between work and worship, we are called to let our work be brought into unity with our worship, becoming part of it.

Living a Holy Life, a Whole Life

In 2007, self-described atheist Hemant Mehta released his provocatively titled book *I Sold my Soul on Ebay*. In it, he describes some of the behaviors of churches and church members across the United States. Among other observations, he identifies a common formula communicated to non-believers or the "lost": "Life is difficult, and each of us needs Jesus to navigate through an existence mired in pain, loss, and hopelessness"—to which Mehta responds: "My life is not painful, hopeless, or difficult. Therefore, according to your formula, I don't need Jesus."

Shortly after the release of Mehta's book, a mega-church pastor presented to his widely-read blog this simple question: "How would you respond to Mehta?" The responses were revealing. Many accused the author of lying. Others suggested that he was more hopeless than he was letting on. Some respondents declared that he will eventually experience loss so great that he would then require Jesus. In other words, Christians want to believe that Mehta will experience or has experienced pain and that he was or will be unhappy enough to turn to Jesus. The implication is that Jesus is the remedy, the key to happiness.

This conversation is interesting. It reflects a longstanding view of faith as being only a means to an end. What is that end? It is happiness. But is happiness really the goal of the Christian faith? Is Jesus only a tool to bring about our happiness on earth and in heaven? Consider an alternative life goal. Instead of seeking happiness, we should strive toward wholeness, toward holiness. If a divided mind and heart, especially in the workplace, is a problem, then wholeness is the necessary solution.

Mehta may not be motivated to seek God in pursuit of wholeness, but Christians should be. What is wholeness? It is arranging, managing, and navigating our lives in a unified manner, or what Ezekiel 11:19 describes as an "undivided heart."

A common story is told among church-goers regarding a confused young girl who confronts her pastor after a Sunday service: "Pastor, you said Jesus should exist inside of us. However, if Jesus was in me, he would be sticking out all over." The pastor considered this comment, smiled, and responded: "Yes, that is right...if Jesus exists in you, He will indeed be sticking out all over." The story's message is clear. The fullness of God should not only be evident to others, but it also should leave little room within us for alternative commitments and contrasting allegiances.

From years of experience in church and in the workplace, we see that too many Christians feel divided, especially as they go to work. Many think we must change our allegiances in order to survive in the workplace. Because the aims of faith at home and church are seemingly different from the expectations at work, we risk a form of spiritual schizophrenia. Christians often try to travel simultaneously along what they view as two different roads: their work and their spirituality. The belief is that one's work life, vocation, job, labor are separate from spiritual essence. However, we submit that this belief leads to a life that is unacceptably divided—unholy.

Our purpose in these pages is to offer a better path—a singular road that lets the faithful Christian be in various work environments and remain undivided. We do not need to divorce our identities. Wholeness does not attempt to dance and fight. It does not "limp." It does not separate the faith life from other important aspects of life. It recognizes that everything we think, say, and do can be an act of worship. This is *holiness*; this is *wholeness*. Being whole is not being totally separated from the presence of sin, pain, or vice; instead, it is being in the full presence of God in the midst of any and all circumstances. Moreover, a singular focus on this divine presence crowds out the space required by

> *Being whole is not being totally separated from the presence of sin, pain, or vice; instead, it is being in the full presence of God in the midst of any and all circumstances.*

other allegiances, and it reflects a life that displays a unified, constant, and consistent act of worship.

Integrity: Living Holy and Whole

In mathematics, we are often confronted with percentages or fractions that give us long, laborious numbers such as 3.27895 or 78.683 percent. However, by rounding up or down we can make such numbers much cleaner, such as 3 or 78. These are called integers or whole numbers. Integers are complete, whole, and consistent. It comes as little surprise, then, that the word "integrity" is derived from the math term "integer."

The word "integrity" is often used in the context of telling the truth. We believe that to have integrity is simply to be honest. While this is true, it is an incomplete use of the word. Integrity is not only about telling the truth, but about being whole and consistent as human beings in all our relationships and activities?

In the Bible, we find no shortage of condemnation for those who are inconsistent, who lack integrity and thus are unholy. Jesus denounces inconsistency when we says, "Out of the abundance of the heart the mouth speaks" (Matt.

12:34), and he directly accuses the Pharisees of spiritual inconsistency (comparing them to "white-washed tombs" in Matthew 23:27). Before Jacob was given a blessing by the angel he wrestled vigorously. He was confronted with his own inconsistent identity. Samson (Judges 16), David (2 Sam. 11), Achan (Joshua 7), Balaam (Num. 22), and Saul (1 Sam.) are just a few noteworthy examples of those whose divided interests ultimately brought shame and hardship to their doorsteps. Moreover, it was God who declared that the "lukewarm" (neither hot nor cold) were about to be spit out of his mouth (Rev. 3:16).

The examples go on and on. The point is that there is a clear biblical trajectory toward consistent and complete living: holiness and wholeness, integrity. Unfortunately, many conflicting forces threaten that trajectory. We shall explore some of these forces in the context of the modern workplace.

Work-Worship Divides

We have to work. There is a duty to be productive and a necessity to earn a living. Our purpose as a Christian is to worship as we undertake life's various activities—including our work. We often work long hours. We have a family to take care of. We have real responsibilities but also want to be godly in them all. This is not merely an academic or theological question to ponder; it is a real and very practical issue and something we should think about on a regular basis. Do you? Are you looking for guidance on the road to integrity in all of your life?

While we work, is it possible to live out our primary identity as Christians? Is it possible to worship at work? Worship is an expression of our primary identity as followers of Jesus Christ that leads to our commitment to "love God and to love others." It is our faith life, our spiritual existence. Worship is not limited to what we do on Sunday or as part of a church service. Worship refers to our core being as Christians. Bringing this into unity with our lives of work is the goal at issue here.

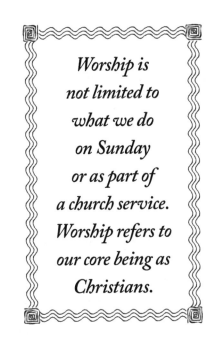

Worship is not limited to what we do on Sunday or as part of a church service. Worship refers to our core being as Christians.

Yet, the reality may be that many of us Christians are divided between work and worship. Because of this unfortunate but common circumstance, we offer four misconceptions about work and worship. Each results in a "divide" that undermines our wholeness and compromises our holiness. As Christians, we know that worship should be part and parcel of all aspects of life. Therefore, none of the following misconceptions are the best fulfillment of holiness and wholeness in the workplace.

Misconception One: Work *not* Worship. The first obvious misconception of the Work-Worship Divide is the separation of work and worship. In this view, the two are both part of our lives, yet essentially unrelated. Christians behave one way on Sunday morning and in a somewhat different way once they head to work on Monday morning.

"I've been sinning all week," a worship leader once announced to a perplexed congregation, "but on this Sunday morning I am here to worship!" We may find such a statement strange coming from a worship leader, but is it any less odd when it comes from the Christian business man or woman? A social worker or nurse? The teacher, store owner, babysitter, or mechanic?

The Work *not* Worship Divide is a false view that assumes that our faith has no bearing on our work identity. We can literally be two or more different people and manage to navigate in and out of these identities as we go about our lives. Among other problems, this assumes that expressions of faith are merely *things we do* (without consideration to *who we are*).

This perspective has infiltrated our language. Take the use of the word "worship." While it is indeed a multi-faceted term in faith circles, its usage primarily relates to the 20-40 minutes of the instrument playing, hymn-singing, hand-clapping, arm-raising activity occurring during a particular portion of a Sunday morning church service. "How is the worship?"—for example—is a common question asked of a church's program. It is curious that this part of the week is understood as worship, suggesting that the rest of the week is something else entirely.

In another sphere, consider the all-too-familiar notion that "business is business" or, worse yet, "it is only business." These phrases are often used as justification for doing things that are considered inappropriate outside the business setting. How does the "business is business" mantra sound in these sentences?

- "I am uncomfortable marketing sexually explicit material, but *business is business.*"
- "I am sorry I have to cheat you—especially after thirty years of friendship, Christmas parties, getting to know each other's families, etc.—but *business is business.*"
- "I know I told you one thing, but the circumstances have changed and *business is business.*"

These statements (which may be all-too-real for some readers) can come off as cold, but that is just the point: work is work, play is play, friends are friends, and faith is faith. These categories (we might say *identities*) are less like mixing paints that bleed together to form a new color. It is really more like a series of silos, freestanding, each possessing its own content. Some authors have referred to this as *privatization*, where one's personal identity has little to no bearing on public identities.

The Work *not* Worship Divide is simple. I am one person at work and another outside of work. Such a person is not whole, and certainly not holy. Do you see this tendency in yourself?

Misconception Two: Work *then* Worship. If the Work *not* Worship Divide inappropriately divorces our faith and work identities, the Work *then* Worship Divide is the attempt to make the two co-exist. Knowing that the first option is not right, we attempt this awkward way of integrating the two, quietly knowing that for us work is really the priority. Many of us know that it is not right to divorce our work and our worship lives. But, in trying to find a way to fit our spiritual self into our work, we may only create another divide.

The Work *then* Worship Divide can come at two levels. At one, it may be as simple as—I am a Christian and I must work. Therefore, I will go and do my job the best I can, making only the compromises that are absolutely necessary. To make this functional, I somehow will need to be "Christian" at work. This means that I will exhibit attributes that I believe represent a Christian commitment. As a way of minimizing any disconnect, I can always revert to a business justification for my Christian characteristics at work. If I am "Christian at work," I hope that I will be blessed and the business will prosper. Such a view runs the risk of using Christianity as a tool for our work ends. The attempt is to integrate Christianity into the workplace, taking Christian principles and trying to make them fit into the work setting the best way we can.

Under this second misconception, glorifying God means showing up to work on time, being punctual, and displaying a general attitude that is considered "nice" and productive. It is amazing how many times well-meaning Christians speculate that a person is a Christian because they are "nice." As attractive as such a quality seems for a workplace, being nice and on time are meant to complement—*not redefine*—our work life.

Being nice may seem good, but it understands our faith life as merely filling in the blanks of our regular life. Author Lee Camp refers to this as the "ethic of vocation" where Christians bring values such as honesty, a good attitude, and a solid work ethic to the worldly structures without questioning the very nature of the social practices inherent in those structures.

Good Christians should do the right thing at work, but is this all there is to being a Christian in the workplace?

In the American culture, Christians have created an economic justification for this view. The ethic of vocation often works. We have come to believe that faith attributes—honesty and prudence, etc., assist us in doing better at work. In other words, being "Christian" will help us be successful. Instead of questioning social structures and economic and political practices, we buy into it the system by thinking we have "the formula" for success. We ask, how successful will we be personally and organizationally if we just act more Christian?

Recently a friend shared the argument that Christian values produce business success. He proclaimed that Christians in his business firm were pitching a "servant leadership" training regimen to upper management because it would ultimately make the company more profitable. But what if it did not make the company more profitable? Should the company still undertake the program? Should servant leadership be promoted because it has a positive consequence for a firm? Or should we advocate such a view of leadership because that it is a character trait that God desires within us?

Knowing where these questions were going, my friend responded that money, in many organizations, is the "language of business." Speaking in that language is necessary for Christians in order to implement faith-driven principles such as servant leadership. While this argument may make sense—to an extent—this view risks making Christian values nothing more than a formula for *profitable performance* in the firm. Whether it is being honest or implementing principles such as servant leadership, their worth is determined by what they produce.

What if the Christian formula for success does not work in dollar terms? The reality is that it does not always work out the way we want. While some people argue that being more Christian leads to profit, there is evidence that this is not always true.

An interesting study conducted by Dan Schafer found that the Christian concept of grace can actually become poison in a Christian organization. Why? Because its misapplication can inhibit management from making personnel decisions necessary for the organization to be effective and efficient in fulfilling its mission. In the for-profit segment of the economy, an interesting example is the experience that Dennis Bakke shares in his book *Joy at Work*. He intentionally created a work culture reflecting his interpretation of Christian values and he was applauded, as long as exceptional profits followed. When those profits waned, the same values that made him a hero cost him his job.

The reality is that the "Christian attribute" formula does not always work in our business or individual lives. We can exhibit the right Christian virtues, work hard, be honest, treat people right, and still fail at our job, be downsized or suffer loss. Do you find yourself heading to work thinking, "I am going to be Christian at work today and I think that God will bless me and the school or company for it?" If so, maybe you are living in the Work *then* Worship divide.

Misconception Three: Work *and* Worship. A third perversion of the *Work-Worship Divide* is the inappropriate mixing of our work and our worship. "And" is used here in the purest sense where we take our work identity and mix it with our faith identity. *Everything is spiritualized.*

Have you ever known a person who in striving to mix two good things and ends up ruining them both? For example, many children enjoy a sugary cereal *and* orange juice. Then comes the faulty logic. If I like orange juice and I like, say, Captain Crunch, then does it not stand to reason that I will like—and perhaps even love—orange juice *in* a bowl of Captain Crunch cereal? It would only take one bite of this odd mixture, however, to realize that this breakfast concoction is not the sum of its parts. The thought alone is enough to conclude that the blending of both would be horrible. Similarly, the inappropriate blending of faith and work risks an equally strange concoction.

First, this misconception risks the over-spiritualization of one's work life. This may not sound like such a bad thing, but in reality it can be a distortion of the faith. Under this paradigm, one might conclude that routine work decisions are a product of *God's will*. Everything, even the smallest of things, is attributed to God's intervention. While we are not rejecting the notion of God's involvement in our lives, this tendency can become an overused and misplaced crutch.

As employees in two Christian universities, we have heard no shortage of stories where day-to-day operational tasks in the workplace or relational challenges are communicated as "God's will"—which means that those who oppose the task or direction find themselves in disagreement not only with co-workers, but supposedly with the Creator of the universe! The risk of using God as a tool for self-justification seems too great. We make everything holier than it deserves to be.

Second, trying to mix worship into work leaves little space for the mundane. We have all heard of faith stories that are miraculous, highly emotional, and utterly spiritual. These moments can appropriately be referred to as "mountain-top experiences." These transformational encounters often comprise the substance of our Christian testimonies. And yet, our life cannot be lived on the mountain indefinitely. Indeed, even after the Transfiguration and against Peter's impulse to create "dwellings" and remain upon the sacred mountaintop, Jesus *came down* from the mountain (Matt. 17:9).

How does this relate to work? Like Peter, as much as we may want to dwell atop the mountains of life, our work activity is very often done in the valleys. Indeed, it is hard to feel immersed in the miraculous when you are constantly changing diapers, entering data, fertilizing a field, disciplining children, designing software, etc. And yet, that is often the nature of our work. The mistake occurs when we think that something is wrong with our work in the valley because it doesn't *feel* like dwelling atop the spiritual mountain.

Without a healthier conception of the mundane, and a more acute understanding of our own spiritual emotions, our faith may only rise to the level of our feelings, and that becomes a challenge when we find ourselves in the valley. What do we do when our faith is not feeling alive in the mundane nature of our work? Do we quit our jobs? That is probably not feasible. Do we quit our faith? Hopefully not!

Finally, the inappropriate accommodation of our work and our worship may lead to exhaustion. If a person attempts to invest fully in a job and church group, have multiple accountability partners, and be responsible for various community engagements and personal devotional lives, it will only be a matter of time until burn-out kicks in. In the study of economics, each semester begins with the simple yet fundamental problem of economics: scarcity. Scarcity is simply the truth that our resources are limited. And yet, we often behave as if our physical and emotional resources are unlimited, and then we act perplexed when we find ourselves sick and weary and doubting our faith.

Unnaturally mixing work with our faith life, where both are placed side-by-side, is to mistakenly give them equal value. While our lives consist of both, work and worship, our work is not equal to our worship. Do you hear yourself trying to spiritualize everything as your way of unifying your faith and your work? Is this "and" driving you to ruin? How is that feeling? Do you sense that something about this must be wrong?

Misconception Four: Work *or* Worship. The final perversion of the Work-Worship Divide occurs when we think we must decide between Christian work or secular work. If the Work *then* Worship paradigm risks understanding the faith life as playing handmaiden to our primary work identity, this misconception risks making "worship" as a vocation that is the only acceptable occupation. Under this way of thinking, as a Christian we have a critical decision to make with vocation: do we take the Christian route and go into ministry (or an acceptable human services field) or take the non-Christian route and go into a secular work field?

A relative who works in an educational ministry recently interviewed a very successful middle-aged financial consultant who was considering a "jump into ministry" from his secular finance job. "I suppose the question is," he pondered out loud, "whether I want my job to allow me to *support* those who are in ministry, or whether I want my job to *be* my ministry." While understandable, we challenge the notion that one field is considered ministry and another is not. Is there only one route by which "work" is worship? Is going into formal ministry or a service profession the only good option? While ministry is work, the Work *or* Worship divide suggests that the only form of legitimate work worthy of true worship is one of ministry or human services.

The Work *or* Worship belief places the majority of us in a less than becoming situation. If we really love God and want our lives to reflect totally our worship, apparently we dare not work in a secular setting or in a non-ministry vocation. Most certainly, we cannot work in the business world. Even if our natural gifts suggest this vocational choice, it is certainly not less desirable. At best, such an occupation is not seen as a "calling." At worst, it may be viewed as a compromise of Christian values. Often a business person is categorically labeled "greedy." The person living under the Work *or* Worship divide, and working in a "less holy" profession, can come to believe that he/she is living a less than optimal life.

Ironically, there is evidence that the Work *or* Worship divide can also create pain for persons in ministry professions, especially for pastors. If a person testifies to being called into ministry and later finds life outside a ministry profession, how is leaving "the calling" to be explained? What if a person goes into formal ministry and is not really equipped for it, or circumstances do not work out as envisioned? How many pastors have felt required to go into ministry because they thought they had to select ministry in order to have acceptable Christian work?

New research, as part of the Sustaining Health and Pastoral Excellence initiative sponsored by the Lilly Endowment, Inc., suggests that many former pastors actually feel relieved when they excuse themselves of the burden

> *Our faith identity, our ministry, and our worship all precede and supersede other identities and work activities. What we do is a function of who we are.*

of thinking their work must be in formal ministry in order for it to be *holy* and for them to be *whole*. Other former pastors, according to Michael Ross of the Pastor's Institute, experience a tremendous sense of loss when they leave ministry and have to explain to others why they are no longer "doing God's work." Consider the embarrassment of being among the "called" and then no longer bearing the positional evidence of the calling. Within religious circles, the Work *or* Worship divide is in danger of leading to a divided life.

Work *or* worship? Is it true that when we decide what to do for "work," are we really deciding to be or not to be "in ministry"? Under the burden of the Work *or* Worship divide and if I am not in ministry, am I a lesser person and have I abandoned true worship? If I am stuck in ministry for whatever reason, I am trapped. There is an absence of wholeness and confusion about holiness.

A Faithful Narrative: Work *as* Worship

If reading this chapter has helped you identify awkward work-worship divides in your own faith and work lives, consider an alternative way. Go to work tomorrow with a new awareness of the divides and how they may be pulling you apart. In pursuit of greater wholeness, a more proper holiness, ponder this more faithful narrative. We call it Work *as* Worship. This phrase is not necessarily new. There have been other books written on this same topic using this phrase (see Mark Russel's book *Work as Worship*) and there is an interesting group called the "Work as Worship Network" that is addressing this same issue. Other attempts have been made to bring together our worship and our work. There seems to be a yearning in the Christian community to address this issue with a new wisdom. We are adding our perspective to the conversation.

As you go to enter into the work environment, consider that it may be inappropriate to divorce faith identity (worship) from other realms of life (work, family, hobbies, etc.). Our faith identity, our ministry, and our worship all precede and supersede other identities and work activities. What we *do* is a function of who we *are*. Obviously, this is the opposite of the work-worship divide.

Work and worship should not be divided, nor should they be inappropriately married. Rather, as followers of Christ, we begin with our faith identity, and then we understand and act in the world based on that identity. Christians are equipped to view, process, and act in the world in a faithful way. In addition to "taking every thought captive and making it obedient to Christ" (2 Cor. 10:5), our activity is to be "salt and light" so that we can "honor and glorify the Lord" (Matt. 5:16). Our identity as Christians, cultivated and refined through the faith community, is our lens through which to perceive and engage the world around us.

Consider your work *as* worship. When working, how can we intentionally make the activity an expression of honor and love to God? How can we live in His presence while at work? What does work *as* worship look like? The answer to these questions will comprise the balance of this book—what we refer to as the 4 C's of Work *as* Worship. These C's are:

- Co-Creation
- Catalyst
- Community
- Contribution

The chapters that follow offer a more detailed picture of how we define and activate Work *as* Worship. By giving attention to aspects of our work as an act of faith, our aim is to shed light on a faithful perspective of what it means to engage the world *with Christ*. It is important to point out that Work *as* Worship does not bring salvation. As a result of the redeeming work of Christ, we receive salvation and strive for the gift of holiness. Moreover, as the Spirit of God shapes us in holiness, we should be motivated to live in integrity, in wholeness, at home, in church, and at work. Our hope is that we can live within the *present fullness* of God in all aspect of our lives.

Reflect for Yourself or for Discussion with Others

1. Do you see any evidence of a "divided heart" in your work life?

2. As you read the divides, the misconceptions, did one of them especially resonate with you? Were there aspects of multiple divides that you can relate to?

3. What is it about your specific work situation that makes you feel divided?

4. What factors outside of work—family, church situation, financial situation, theology—contribute in your understanding of work? How are these relieving or feeding your sense of a work/worship divide?

5. Do you really want to see your Work *as* Worship? What benefits for you, your family, and your service to God do you see coming if you would change your orientation to your work?

CHAPTER 2

Co-creators with God

To be "holy" is to work with and for God.

Thus far, we have outlined the problems with a divided self—specifically in the context of the relationship between our work life and our faith life. In contrast to the previously identified work-worship divides, we call for a more faithful concept of our work lives. As Christians, our approach to work—or any other facet of our lives—should be undivided, consistent, whole, holy.

The upcoming chapters will provide a different way of thinking about work as a Christian. When we go to work, we can be—should be—worshipping. How so? There are four ways that this is to be true—what we refer to as the four Cs.

Co-Creating with God (this chapter)
Catalyst for our God-given gifts (chapter three)

Creating Community (chapter four)

Contribution to God's Kingdom (chapter five)

As we consider the ways that we can make work into worship, two verses serve as our biblical focus. The first is Ephesians 2:10, "we are God's workmanship, created in Christ Jesus to do good works, which God prepared in advance for us to do" (NIV). Salvation does not come from our work, even Work *as* Worship, but as Christians we need to acknowledge that we have a purpose and that we are designed by God for "good works." The reality of the workplace can undermine our resolve. As humans, it is a challenge to make our work worship. Thankfully, there is hope. Romans 12:1-2 reminds us that it will take a spiritual renewal of our mind.

Therefore, I urge you, brothers and sisters, in view of God's mercy, to offer your bodies as a living sacrifice, holy and pleasing to God—this is your true and proper worship.[2] Do not conform to the pattern of this world, but be transformed by the renewing of your mind. Then you will be able to test and approve what God's will is—his good, pleasing and perfect will.

Work *as* Worship requires a "renewal of our minds." The divides discussed in chapter one are attempts to conform to the "pattern of this world," both the secular and the religious ones. To make our work experience an act of worship, to be a "living sacrifice, holy and pleasing to God," we will need to change our mind. This call is not to do more. It is to be different in what we do. As we ask God's Spirit to "renew our minds," we may discover how to make our work an act of worship.

Before we begin, one expectation needs to be established (this will be repeated at the beginning of each chapter). We are not advocating a specific formula that you can apply automatically get what you want. Work *as* Worship is not a 1-2-3 step process; a just do this and "now you have it" plan. As Romans 12:2 calls for, Work *as* Worship is a mindset, an attitude. As you adjust your way of thinking about your work, you will find God doing a divine work in you. So, our expectation of you as the reader is not to "figure it out." Instead, allow your focus to be *on God*, so that your work, whatever it is, becomes true worship.

The focus of this chapter is the co-creating role we play as we work. When you go to work as a Christian, you are offered an opportunity by God to co-create with the divine. A holy life calls us to be in alignment with the activity of God. In this chapter we will explore three ways in which work is an act of co-creation. First, identify how what you are doing fits into the big picture of what your organization is doing. Second, embrace your work as a creative process. Third, accept the *essence* of what you do, not simply the *necessity* of it.

The framework of Work *as* Worship understands our work activity as joining with God's creative process to bring about His will and way on earth. Let us learn more about being *co-creators* with God through our work.

Shaping Stones or Building Cathedrals?

Why do we work? You may simply answer that it is because we have to. We sell our effort, skill, and ability—both physical and mental—in the labor market and we use the wages we earn to maintain a living. This exchange—labor for income—summarizes the economics of the labor market. Yet, is this all there is? Do we work and produce simply to survive? Maybe, as a Christian, our work, toil, and labor is much larger reality than we often understand. To illustrate, consider this familiar story.

In the days of misty towers, distressed maidens and stalwart knights, a young man, walking down a road came upon a laborer fiercely pounding away at a stone with hammer and chisel. The lad asked the worker, who looked frustrated and angry, "What are you doing?" The laborer answered in a pained voice: "I'm trying to shape this stone and it is backbreaking work." The youth continued his journey and soon came upon another man chipping away at a similar stone. This man looked neither particularly angry nor happy. "What are you doing," he asked? "I'm shaping a stone for a building." The young man went on and before long came to a third worker chipping away at a stone, but this worker was singing happily as he worked. "What are you doing?" The worker smiled and replied, "I'm building a cathedral."[1]

It is likely that you are familiar with a friend, employee, or acquaintance whose toil, it would seem, involves nothing more than the hard labor of shaping stones. Maybe you feel this way yourself. In contrast, it is likely that we are equally familiar with those whose work reflects a deeper motivation than merely earning a living. These individuals take joy in what they do. They are creative, inspired, and passionate. Their work gets them out of the bed in the morning. They do not shape stones—they *build cathedrals*.

What are we to make of this difference? Is your work just a task to be done in order to produce a paycheck? Are you just shaping stones where you work? Or is what you do part of the creative process that will lead to something worthwhile and useful? Are you building a cathedral?

In reality, work can easily be engaged in with a mundane sense of only earning a living. Work can be an obligation; that is to say, it is necessary for survival. Work, even if mundane or unpleasant, is often appropriately viewed as a means to an end. One's labor provides a wage, which in turn gives us an opportunity for shelter, food, and clothing. Further, our wage allows us to satisfy our preferences in the marketplace (purchasing a good book, buying food, funding a vacation, etc.).

While this is all true, such a framework of thought risks making our work only something that *we do*—disconnected to from *who we are*. As Christians, the view that we are only shaping stones can lead to the various work-worship divides discussed in chapter one. Work that is merely a means to an end, especially when the work is not that gratifying, can be dehumanizing. For example, there was a particular grocery store worker who proclaimed the same thing every morning as he clocked in for his shift: "dead until 3:00." For him, his life ended when he went to work and restarted when he got off work.

> *Are you just shaping stones where you work? Or is what you do understood to be part of a creative process that will lead to something worthwhile and useful? In other words, are you building a cathedral with your stones?*

Changing our focus to Work *as* Worship, let us consider engaging work as a creative statement. Work is an expression. For Christians, this expression is worship. It is an extension of who we are as Christ's children and his co-laborers. We become the engaged mason whose end purpose is to build a cathedral—with his manual labor not simply a means to an end, but viewed as a distinct form of *participation* in something much greater than himself. As cathedral builders, our work becomes a function of who we are, and it is a part of our spiritual legacy. While the actual work may be forming stone, we are not producing, working, and laboring as a mere means to live. Rather, our daily life (identity, creativity, personhood) is bound up in making our work an act of devotion to God.

Work as Creative Despite Cultural Trends

David Kinnaman, president of the Barna Group, has given recent attention to several cultural trends characteristic of today's society and pivotal for determining wise church life. Among other things, his research attends to our modern perceptions of work—and what he has found is not encouraging.

Looking specifically at youth and young adults (18-29 years old), Kinnaman has found a discernible disconnect between vocational desire and faith identity. In his recent book, *You Lost Me*, he writes: "Millions of Christ-following teens and young adults are interested in serving in mainstream professions…. Yet most receive little guidance from their church communities for how to connect these vocational dreams deeply with their faith in Christ."[2] As a result, many Christians in their 20s fail to link their career choices and their approach to work with a sense of calling. The result? Their "faith and work decisions are bifurcated rather than holistically entwined."[3]

This "bifurcation" is not limited to young adults. Consider a 2012 survey done by *Salary.com* which found that only 19% of working adults would characterize themselves as "living to work" while 70% would characterize their activity as "working to live."[4] It is little surprise, then, that a Gallup Poll conducted the same year found that less than half of all workers in the United States considered themselves "completely satisfied" with their job, with the majority indicating that they are only somewhat satisfied or even dissatisfied. Furthermore, the study found that working adults were least satisfied with their stress-load at work as well as their pay.[5]

One might think that these statistics merely reflect job dissatisfaction—something not that uncommon. This is true, and the process of sorting and re-sorting in the U. S. labor market is a good thing because, ultimately, it means that individuals are self-selecting into jobs that better match their skills, talents, abilities, and passions. Yet the reality is that many people feel stuck in jobs and, consequently, do not feel the freedom to do something else. It is easy to understand how job dissatisfaction and a "working to live" mentality risk more than simply producing a disengaged worker; they risk fostering a "shaping stone" mentality.

In contrast, consider Paul's powerful words written to Christian servants: "Whatever you do, work at it with all your heart, as working for the Lord, not for human masters" (Col. 3:23). Paul begins this passage by addressing wives, husbands, children and parents, but ends with the suggestion that, even if you find yourself in a master-servant arrangement, you should do your work *heartily* as if working and creating in a way that glorifies the grand Creator (and not merely for a human employer). This verse is not meant to suggest that we simply accept the status quo of distasteful social conventions (such as slavery); it does imply that in our work, whatever it may be at a given time, we have an opportunity to create and *worship*.

Many adults do not live under such a paradigm. Moreover, in the greater Christian faith community, our next generation of workers appear no different. Kinnaman summarizes the problem well. Millions of next-generation Christians "have no idea that their faith connects to their life's work."[6]

Necessary Work or the Essence of Life?

While the story of the working masons is likely mere fiction, it offers a very real description of what it means to worship in and through our labor—Work *as* Worship. To understand this, we need to see the difference between these two conceptions of work: shaping stones and building cathedrals. We will refer to the former as producing to survive—or *necessary labor*. Similarly, we will refer to the latter, producing to worship, as *essence labor*.

Necessary labor is a means to an end. As suggested,

the end we speak of is based simply, and perhaps solely, on what is produced. To be clear, we make no claim that such motivations are morally wrong. However, this singular conception of work risks the *Work-Worship* divisions referenced earlier.

What is morally questionable, however, is the belief that our work—understood as a means to an end—is sufficient to satisfy our deepest human desire for fulfillment. In his book *God the Economist*, Douglas Meeks writes: "God's gracious justification means that no one must justify himself or herself through work nor does anyone have to create or realize him or herself through work."[7] Our labor, if understood as a means to an end, risks making our value as human beings—as children of God—contingent on what we produce. "She is very successful," we remark, "She has a six-figure salary." Or consider the opposite: "He is a failure—He can't hold down a job." In our society, we tend to evaluate each other in this rather rigid form of produce and gain. While this makes sense in our everyday culture, is this really biblical? Does God value us merely because of what we produce and reward us because of what we have produced?

In contrast, essence labor is not a means to an end. It views work in a wider, more morally rich and meaningful way. Our labor is not just what we do, but an illustration—a picture—of who we are, and more importantly, *whose* we are. Indeed, essence labor reflects upon something—or someone—outside of us. For Christians, what we do is a light unto the world (Matt. 5:14). The purpose of this light is not to highlight and draw greater attention to ourselves—it is meant to ultimately point others to God (Matt. 5:16).

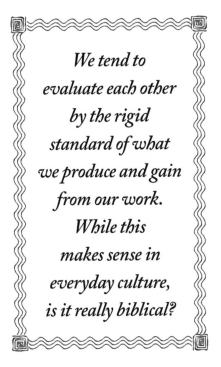

We tend to evaluate each other by the rigid standard of what we produce and gain from our work. While this makes sense in everyday culture, is it really biblical?

Essence labor contrasts sharply with necessary labor in that a person's worth is not bound up in the value of what is produced. Our very work (apart from what comes out on the other end) is an expression in itself; it is an act of worship. To provide an example of this, Anderson University was fortunate to have former all-star baseball pitcher Carl Erskine as the commencement speaker for the 2011-2012 school year.[8] In his address, Erskine—whose son Jimmy has Down Syndrome—described the Special Olympics and the unique nature of its events.

"In a race, the first-place winner gets a rousing applause from the audience," Erskine recalled. "But the very last runner in that same race, the one who is often one to two minutes behind, gets the loudest applause of all!"

This moving picture of a Special Olympics race illuminates the very heart of essence labor: we are valued not for what we produce, but for who we are. Therefore, embracing and embodying essence labor requires a strong sense of the identity of God in us and working through us. But what, exactly, does this mean? What is it about the identity of God that allows us to be "co-creators?"

Co-Creators with God

A prominent philosopher, upon reviewing the Genesis narrative, once asked: "If God is all-sufficient and lacks nothing, how does he come to release himself into something so utterly unequal to him?"[9] In other words, why did God create a world—and a people to inhabit this world—if he is indeed all-sufficient? Why does a God who does not need anything seem to need people?

While this philosopher constructed an answer to his own question, there is an alternative answer to consider, particularly from believers who subscribe to God as creator. Instead of directly asking "why" God created the world and humankind to inhabit it, we might better get at the truth by inserting "what" into the inquiry. That is, what does it tell us about God, the God who created the world and human beings in the first place? What does this tell us about his nature? In answering the "what" we may gain new clarity and perspective as to the question of "why."

Among other things, we see from the Genesis narrative an important characteristic of God. He is a *creator*. Is God done creating? Todd Bouldin helpfully connects the creative process of God with our work. He points out that the Hebrew verb "create" in Genesis 1:1 can be translated "God began to create the heavens and the earth" and that the creative work of God "continues throughout time." He points out that in Genesis 1:26-28 "God called human creation to be co-creators with him in perfecting and managing the creative order." Bouldin goes on to say,

> ...regardless of the work to which we are called or find ourselves doing, all human beings have the same job description, "Be fruitful and multiply, and fill the earth and subdue it." ...God has assigned us to act as stewards of the creation, [and] the steward's responsibility is not to return something merely the way she found it, but to return a profit for the Lord, making the creation better than she found it.[10]

The perspective of being "co-creator" may provide readers with a new perspective of the Parable of Talents (Matt. 25:14-30). In the parable, the master (God) gave his servants (us) dominion over his resources and asked us to manage them. Two of the servants used the resources creatively and produced a better outcome. The third, in fear, hid the resources and produced nothing new. The master was pleased with the first two, not necessarily because of the size of the outcome but because they were creative in multiplying the resources. The third, however, earned the scorn of the master for lacking creativity and failing to bring about

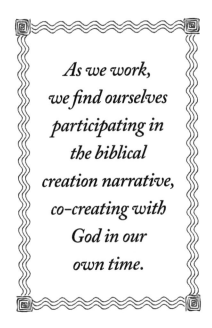

As we work, we find ourselves participating in the biblical creation narrative, co-creating with God in our own time.

good results. That is to say, the third servant did not create anything.

When we go to work, maybe we are being asked by God to invest his co-creating resources for his glory. We are his image-bearers (*Imago Dei*). As God created us, can we become co-creators with him as we work? Scripture suggests that this is God's intention for us. In Romans 8-19-21 Paul calls on the children of God to deliver the creation from the bondage of corruption into a glorious liberty. God continues in his creating, redeeming work. And he asks us to be his active agents in the creating process. Jesus tells us to be to be his "salt and light" and lets us know that we really serve no purpose if we lose our "saltiness" (Matt. 5:13-16).

As we work, we find ourselves participating in the creation narrative and co-creating with God. Thus, work, creativity, and production are not merely appreciated for their extrinsic value (i.e., the nature of what is produced) or what we have referred to as necessary labor, but also for their intrinsic value (capitalizing on the attributes of God inherent in our being)—what we have called essence labor. To be specific, when I create something, it is a form of worship because I am reflecting God's nature inherent in me as his image-bearer: I am co-creating with God. To be "holy" is to work with and for God.

Image Bearers of a Creative God

In 2006, acclaimed author Cormac McCarthy wrote *The Road*, a novel depicting a father-son duo trying to navigate a post-apocalyptic world. The story, which the *New York Times* described as offering "nothing in the way of escape or comfort, details their grisly journey to warmer and safer terrain amidst gloomy weather and even gloomier strangers who threaten their survival.[11]

Struggling to press forward despite limited food, ragged clothing, and infrequent shelter, the coarse and hardened father and his innocent son must manage to evade violent, cannibalistic predators whose means for survival involved attacking other, more vulnerable human beings.

Upon first glance, this book appears to be about survival. However, once drawn in, a deeper story emerges. The son, a mere adolescent, is troubled by the notion of survival at all costs. Despite their woeful circumstances, he continues to press his father with questions—not necessarily related to what they are doing (i.e., their plan), but with questions about *who they are* (their virtue and humanity): "Are we still considered good guys?" Among other things, one theme from the book becomes clear. If the world were stripped of all its modern features, would life simply be about survival or would there continue to be an essence to human relations, dignity, and decisions regarding right and wrong? In other words, is surviving and existing the only juice that comes out of squeezing life's fruit?

This is a question worth contemplating. If we distill work and labor down to their bare features, are they only about producing? Should labor, at its core, be understood solely as a means to some end? Is it merely shaping stone? Or, alternatively, is there an essence to work that is intrinsic to its exercise and closely tied to our nature and identity? Is our labor a creative extension of God's work in our lives? Is it worship? Is there a holiness embodied in the process?

Work is more than what we do (our output). Saying this does not dismiss the fact that it is "output" and that producing is valuable in itself. Indeed, work is naturally a part of our "daily bread." We work to earn, to save, and to give. We work to pay our bills, to buy our clothes, to pump our gas, and to feed our families. We work to sustain our yard, to fix what is broken, and to assist those who need our help. In a word, our work is often considered *necessary*. It produces valuable outcomes for practical purposes.

However, there is more to work than what we *do*—work is also an expression of who we *are*. As Christians, our activity has an essence: we create; we relate. And all the while, we reflect our Creator as image-bearers of the divine name and nature. To put it bluntly, when we work we co-create with God. We participate in the divine nature. We find ourselves drawn into something larger than ourselves (e.g., building cathedrals).

Moreover, reflecting God's image—letting our light so shine so as to glorify God—is a distinct form of worship. This is the first "C" of the Work *as* Worship paradigm: Co-Creators with God.

Personalize It

Have you noticed a common conversation starter when you meet new people? We tend to ask, "What do you do for a living?" We now are asking you that question. What do you do for a living? Do you make something? Do you provide a service? Is the nature of the work you do interacting with people, processes, computers, paper, and/or products? At the end of the day, what have you produced?

We are not asking how productive you are or how much money you make or produce for the firm. We are asking a bigger question. What is the actual outcome of your work? Is it a well-made product that someone wants to buy? Is something fixed due to your efforts? Is someone better off or is a problem solved? What is it that you do? How is it related to who you are?

If the God that you love is by nature a creating God, and if God has asked you to align with his redeeming mission as his child, what does that make your work? Worship! If so, how is what you are doing an extension of God's creative and redeeming nature? Is the work you are doing actually an opportunity to demonstrate to God how much you love him and want to serve his purposes?

What do we do for a living? The two of us writing this book are university professors. What does being a co-creator with God mean in our line of work? If you look at the "necessary" work, this job of yours is not very important. We read, research, prepare class material, work with students and student groups, design, give and grade exams and papers, go to meetings and work on departmental issues. Some of this work is not fun. It can be tedious and at times there are conflicts and frustrations. While it is definitely a "good job," the necessary labor is not that glamorous.

But, with a "renewing of the mind" and a consideration of "essence labor," the importance of what we do becomes clear. We are partners with students helping them discover their vocation and prepare for a life of service. We are being used by God to inform, encourage, coach, discipline, befriend and support the development of other people. We are making a difference in the lives of people and our students are having a positive influence on families, churches, places of employment and society as a whole. The feedback from former students tells us that what we do matters. If we enter into our Work *as* Worship, we become privileged to be co-creators with God in helping to shape the future destiny of people and organizations. What we do matters!

For us, as teachers, this means that we need to seek constructive connections with students and colleagues and see them as gifts from God to us and opportunities for us to work and worship. As we deal with the challenges of education, we are worshiping God and finding ways to let God's creative gifts be extended through us. Do not get us wrong. It is not easy and it is not always fun. But, the change in framework does change our attitude and our behavior.

With Work *as* Worship, we need to continually find ways to better connect with students and to assist them to receive and use pertinent material. It calls us to grow, to change, to explore and experiment. We need to work to remain relevant and to make sure that our material and our programs are effective and current. We cannot rest on our laurels. There is need to recreate ourselves, to stay up-to-date and effective.

To settle on what worked before, as long as the paycheck keeps coming, is to see work from the necessary labor perspective. We may be able to get away with it, but is it true worship? Is it right? When we view our work as essence labor, the preparation, the class time, the interactions with students, the research are all forms of worshiping God. As we "do all things as unto the Lord," we cannot help but strive to give our best to God. New creativity is birthed and God is glorified. God uses us to find new ways of doing things, gives us new insights, helps us create new methods and thoughts and, in the end, get better at what we are doing. Work becomes worship.

Sharing some of these thoughts in a Sunday school class recently, a person was struggling to see that what she did matters. Her focus was on the job she does, which is filing governmental documents. Frankly, to her, it was not important and she had no idea how to make filing an act of worship. She stated her frustration and another person in the class, a law enforcement officer, voiced his strong objection to her lacking a sense of worth in her work. He explained what would happen to legal cases if she did not do her job well. As she saw "the big picture," her attitude changed and she was affirmed, even inspired. Her job did matter! With a renewed sense of importance, she expressed her desire to do the job of filing with a new attitude, one of worship that supports the enabling of justice in this world. What about you and your work?

Reflect for Yourself or for Discussion with Others

1. What is your perspective on your daily work? Is it laying stones or building a cathedral?

2. What is the essence of your work? What is it that you "create?"

3. Where are the opportunities for creativity in your workplace? How are you allowed to create, share new ideas, improve what you do and how you do it?

4. What specific ideas do you have for making your work an act of co-creation? What can you improve? What suggestions can you offer? How is it that you can do your job better or more efficiently?

5. How can you make an improvement/contribution to the "essence" of your work and give that as an offering to God?

ENDNOTES

1 Brian Dumaine, "Why Do We Work?" *CNNMoney*. Cable News Network, 26 Dec. 1994. Web. Jan. 2013.

2 David Kinnaman and Aly Hawkins, *You Lost Me: Why Young Christians Are Leaving Church– and Rethinking Faith* (Grand Rapids, MI: Baker, 2011), 29.

3 Ibid., 144.

4 Aaron Gouevia, "Do Americans Still Value Hard Work?" *Salary.com*, 2012. Web. Feb. 2013.

5 "U. S. Workers Least Happy With Their Work Stress and Pay." *U.S. Workers Least Happy With Their Work Stress and Pay.* Gallup.com, 12 Nov. 2012. Web. 22 Feb. 2013.

6 Kinnaman, 2011, 207.

7 M. Douglas Meeks. *God the Economist: The Doctrine of God and Political Economy.* Minneapolis: Fortress, 1989, 149.

8 Erskine was the commencement speaker at Anderson University for the 2011-2012 school year.

9 Hegel in Cohen. See G. A. Cohen, *If You're an Egalitarian, How Come You're so Rich?* (Cambridge, MA: Harvard Univ. Press, 2000), 83.

10 Todd Bouldin, "Co-Workers with God," in *New Wineskins*–The Believers' Magazine, April, 2003. Web, 24 May, 2013.

11 Janet Maslin, "BOOKS OF THE TIMES; The Road Through Hell, Paved With Desperation," *The New York Times,* Sept. 25, 2006.

CHAPTER 3

Being a Catalyst

Engaging one's giftedness is to be holy and whole.

The last chapter invited us to look at the essence of our labor, not simply its necessity. Developing our understanding of the essence of our labor can unleash creative opportunities. We can be co-creators with God.

In this chapter, we add an additional perspective of *Work as Worship*. We are the catalyst for God's work. When we go to work, we take our abilities, talents, and skills with us. When you were hired, you were chosen for your character, abilities, knowledge, and gifts. We have been "gifted" to do something in the workplace. In this chapter we explore what it means to be used in a way that honors God. When God created us, he gifted us. How can and should our giftedness serve as a catalyst to activate God's work through our lives. God has offered us an opportunity to be a catalyst through our work. We can help bring about the divine kingdom.

You Possess a Unique Giftedness

What do we mean by "giftedness"? It is the total set of God-given and developed abilities that are unique to each person and that enable the person to do her/his work. Created by God, we have been given abilities. You are a package of character, personality, skills, knowledge, talents, and gifts. For example, most of us are naturally good at something. We were created by God and made that way. Each of us has also developed and fine-tuned the natural gifts and developed further our skills and aptitudes. Through practice and hard work, we have become good at an array of tasks. Importantly, we have also been endowed by God with spiritual gifts or "graces" that God has bestowed on us to fit into God's plan for use in the divine kingdom. This "total package" is what we are referring to as giftedness.

There is a need for your God-given giftedness to be unleashed in the workplace. Offering it to God is an act of worship. Our gifts can be a catalyst for showing God's glory. How can we let God "fan into flame" the gifts we have been endowed with, or as John Wesley described it, "blowing up the coals into a flame"? To do so, we suggest that Christians can (1) discover their personal God-given giftedness, (2) focus the use of gifts for "God's pleasure" and (3) explore how giftedness can be employed appropriately as an act of stewardship. When we allow our gifts to be catalysts for God, we can become aware of how God is using us as his created handiwork to serve his loving and redeeming purposes.

Again, we need to set expectations. This chapter is less about "gifts" and more about our attitude or mindset about the giftedness that we have been given. As such, the focus is not about "doing the steps" to Work *as* Worship. It is not a formula. We do not want to fall into a "works mentality." In this chapter, then, focus on what *God is doing in us*. Pray about it. Let God lead you to work and worship.

Discover Your Personal God-given Giftedness

Our giftedness says something to others about who we are. That is why, when we are asked "Would you tell me about yourself?" we respond, "Well, I play drums for my church worship team" or "I am a district manager for a Fortune 500 company" or "I am a stay-at-home parent." In other words, in telling people who we *are*, we like to tell them what we *do*. Moreover, in telling people what we do, we are telling them something about our skills, abilities, and talents. To say that you are an author, a nurse, a construction worker, a pastor, a teacher, a programmer, etc., is to say something about the use of your gifts and how they connect to your identity.

It is important to understand our giftedness and how that cherished resource can be employed at work. You may be saying, "I know my gifts and there are no opportunities to use them in my job." For example, a woman might consider herself to be an athlete or a musician. But she finds herself working as a school administrator, or factory worker, or administrative assistant. This is a problem if you have a passion for using a gift, but no apparent opportunity. Frustration, maybe resentment, is often the result.

Often students say that they want a career as a musician. Many times they strongly believe that they are called by God to be a performer. In the end, very few get the opportunities to fulfill this vision. But the innate creativity, the personal presence, the enthusiasm for doing something well—all core qualities for a performer—are at the center of what made them a musician. Even if they are not "on stage" in the job, these God-given qualities can be a catalyst for God using them in the workplace. Years later, these students often come back to tell of how God has used their giftedness to serve fulfilling careers in business, not-for-profits, teaching, or even inventing—even though they never directly used what they thought was their "gift" as part of their work.

The giftedness we have is not always what is seen by others. The "total set" of qualities are unique to you. It is what God's created in you. So, understanding the essence of your giftedness is very important. Once you do, potential is unleashed. You can become a catalyst.

Fortunately, many assessment tools are available today to help you discern your gifts and skills. For example, a popular tool is *StrengthFinder* by Tom Rath. There are also personality assessments, spiritual gifts tests, and career aptitude assessments. In today's marketplace, there are many organizations that specialize in skill, gift, or personal assessments. If you want a better sense of your giftedness, there are resources to help you.

Perhaps you have given serious consideration to your gift-edness. On the other hand, maybe the exploration of your giftedness is an adventure you need to start. In a recent Sunday school class, we were discussing how to better engage the college-aged youth attending our church. One of the adults remarked: "When I was in college, my primary question was, 'Who am I?' To answer this, I was constantly filling out personality inventories to determine what I liked and what I was good at." Many people ask this same question and the tools are used to help them understand who they are.

However, this approach requires caution. In our society, there can be a misplaced fixation on skills and strengths. A society focused too much on skills is a society probably focused too much on *results*. If a person is talented or has high character/quality, such attributes, we assume, will be found in outcomes and results. This logic works backwards too. If a result is poor, then the person, school, business, etc., must not be very good. A daughter comes home from a basketball game only to be met with an array of outcome-based questions: "Did you win?" "How many points did you score?" Or consider a recent college graduate just entering the workforce being asked: "What is your title?" "Is the pay good?" Perhaps you have heard some other results-focused questions: "What is your GPA?" "Did you win the race?" "How many people attend your church?" "What neighborhood do you live in?" "What model of car do you drive?"

These questions are not inherently bad. However, they each imply that the value of a person is solely wrapped up in the results they produce, their performances and outcomes, and their accumulated possessions. We do this in church too. It happens in most churches each week when we ask at dinner, "How was the worship today?" "Did you like the sermon?" Often times the nature of the conversation is about how good the singers sang, if we liked the song selection, and whether or not people had the desired emotional connection. We have a tendency to judge the quality of the giftedness by our preferred results. We all know that a worship leader's career will rise or fall on the assessed quality of performance in relation to our expectations and preferences.

If we are truly working as an act of worship, it is not so much a matter of who has the best gifts or who is getting the most of some desired outcome from the gifts. It is more whether your unique you—your giftedness—is being offered up, honestly, before God as an act of worship. Are you, as much as humanly possible, "a sacrifice of praise?" Is your giftedness a catalyst for worship in your church and workplace?

Having a New Perspective

Enjoy and Employ. Over this last holiday season, a father shared a story relating to Christmas morning with his family. Having young children, he recalled with delight how they exploded out of bed on Christmas day, rushed down the stairs, and enthusiastically opened presents. Later in the day one of the children asked him, "Dad, what was your favorite gift?" After considering this, he replied, "My greatest gift today was watching you and your siblings open yours."

It is not unreasonable to imagine that God is any different. Indeed, God "delights in the well-being of his servant" (Psalm 35:27), gains pleasure from "those who hope in his steadfast love" (Psalm 147:11), and takes delight in his people (Psalm 149:4). Since God is the grand Gift-giver, why would he not also take pleasure when we enjoy the gifts he endows us with? And we certainly know that his gifts are "good" (Matt. 7:11).

However, the legacy of our giftedness relates to its employment, not simply its enjoyment. To provide an example, consider the lyrics

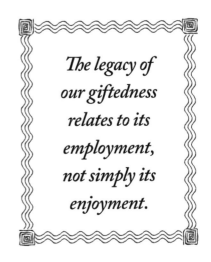

The legacy of our giftedness relates to its employment, not simply its enjoyment.

to the carol "Little Drummer Boy." Originally called "Carol of the Drum," the song was written prior to World War II by Katherine Davis after she found herself "thinking about gifts and how hard it was for people to buy them during the great depression."[1] The song, which has been performed by a multitude of artists since being written, imagines a poor child visiting baby Jesus in Bethlehem. Possessing nothing but a drum, the boy recognizes that he is before a king. Having no possessions worthy of giving a king, he capitalizes on his primary possession. He plays his drum. He employs his gift.

"I played my drums for him. *I played my best for him.*" And what was the king's response? "Then he smiled at me...me and my drum." What a beautiful picture of not simply enjoying one's gift (musical talent), but employing it. While playing his drum, he was displaying his total giftedness, bringing his personal essence to the moment, worshipping.

Seeing a gift *enjoyed* is a delight to its provider, but seeing giftedness *employed* will leave a legacy of the gift's meaningfulness. How should we use our giftedness? We have suggested that gifts are meant to be enjoyed and employed—both of which bring delight to the gift-giver. Giftedness employed is a catalyst for God's work.

Working for God's Pleasure. Our giftedness can be used for personal glory or for God's glory. It is easy to get caught up in "what we are good at" and think that our gifts are given for our own purposes. As Christians, this is simply not true. The gifts were given by God for a purpose. In the workplace, some people are better at some things than others. The focus is not to be on who has the better gifts, but on how the gifts are being employed.

A powerful true story illustrates the difference between using gifts for "self-regard" or for "God's pleasure." Shortly after the 1981 movie *Chariots of Fire* celebrated its 30th anniversary in 2011, director Hugh Hudson suggested that the story is timeless. The movie explores issues relating to purpose, meaning, and destiny—themes that are central to human existence. The story contrasts two world-class runners. Both had been endowed with the ability to run, but each had a different perspective on how the gift was to be used. In one case, the runner's total giftedness was used, not only to win a race, but as a catalyst to serve God's purpose. For the other person, the gift of running was used for self only and it failed to lead to fulfillment.

The two characters are Scotsman Eric Liddell and Cambridge student Harold Abrahams. Liddell is a Christian devoted to his faith and committed to living a life glorifying to God. Abrahams is committed to a different purpose. He is determined to win an Olympic metal. At one point in the movie he admits that running for him is an addiction, a compulsion. Upon being asked how he felt about losing, Abrahams answers: "I don't know...I've never lost."

Liddell was born to missionary parents and felt a call to return to China as a missionary. But one of his gifts was to run. It was a God-given ability that was fine-tuned to the point that he was capable of competing in the Olympics. While Lindell saw his life purpose as a missionary to China, he also saw an opportunity to use his gift as a runner to compete in the Olympics. His sister, Jenny, thought this was a recipe for conflict. In the film, she confronts him about his participation in the 1924 Olympics and expresses her disapproval of his participation in what she considered a distraction to God's purpose for Liddell. Liddell responds to his sister's concerns: "Jenny, I believe God made me for a purpose [China], but he also made me fast. And when I run, *I feel his pleasure.*"

This is a thought-provoking statement. Liddell's character in the movie makes a distinction between pleasing God by doing his work (purpose) and pleasing God by exercising, demonstrating, and reflecting the gifts and attributes God has endowed us with. Liddell had many gifts, one of which was running; and in utilizing this gift, he was glorifying the gift-giver.

In one scene, after winning another race, Liddell addresses a crowd eager to hear him speak. He explains how a gift, running, is only part of his total giftedness and how his identity as a Christian is used by God to be a catalyst for kingdom work:

> You came to see a race today...to see someone win. It happened to be me. But I want you to do more than just watch a race. I want you to take part in it. I want to compare faith to running in a race. It's hard. It requires concentration of will, energy of soul. You experience elation when the winner breaks the tape, especially if you've got a bet on it. But how long does that last? You go home. Maybe your dinner is burnt. Maybe you haven't got a job. So who am I to say, "Believe, have faith," in the face of life's realities? I would like to give you something more permanent, but I can only point the way. I have no formula for winning the race. Everyone runs in her own way, or his own way. And where does the power come from to see the race to its end? From within. Jesus said, "Behold, the kingdom of God is within you. If with all your

hearts you truly seek me, you shall ever surely find me." If you commit yourself to the love of Christ, then that is how you run a straight race.

Liddell had a gift of running, but he employed his giftedness in a way that helped others to see a larger picture: "I want you to do more than just watch a race." He was called to China, but he used his gift of running to be faithful where he was at that given time. Liddell's gift was not solely for himself and his own purposes. He "let his light shine" so that it ultimately pointed back to the Master.

Apply the idea of "God's pleasure" to the work setting that you know. Like Liddell, perhaps you have not yet reached your destination, but you still have giftedness to use. Using your giftedness in the setting where you happen to find yourself gives you an opportunity to be used as a catalyst for God's blessing on your life and for "his pleasure." On the other hand, maybe you find yourself exactly where you believe God intends you to be. The same principle holds true. Your giftedness is to be dispensed for "God's pleasure." Regardless of the setting or situation, it is an opportunity for God to be worshipped and served. You are to be—and can be—a catalyst for bringing that opportunity to reality.

This is made even more apparent in the contrasting perspective of the other runner, Abrahams. He was also blessed with the gift of running. When confronted with his ultimate goal, the 1924 Olympics in Paris, he began to have doubts. Speaking to one of his teammates, Aubrey, he offers this poignant confession:

> You, Aubrey, are my most complete man. You're brave, compassionate, kind: a content man. That is your secret: contentment. I am 24 and I've never known it. I'm forever in pursuit and I don't even know what I'm chasing. And now in one hour's time I will be out there again. I will raise my eyes and look down that corridor, four feet wide, with ten lonely seconds to justify my whole existence. But will I? Aubrey, I've known the fear of losing but now I am almost too frightened to win.

Abrahams had embraced and enjoyed his gift, running. Further, he employed it. He cultivated this skill through practice and training accompanied by a dogged determination to succeed. However, as this quote makes evident, he employed this gift for himself. There was emptiness inside him. He wrongly assumed that the void within would be filled—that he would be fulfilled—upon achieving gold in an Olympic race ("with ten lonely seconds to justify my whole existence").

The fate of Abrahams is all too familiar in the work world. We all know highly gifted and ambitious people who sacrifice much to "succeed." Yet, in the end, they are left empty. Their gifts have been employed for the wrong purpose. They were created to use their skill set in a way that is glorifying to God, the gift-giver. Instead, their entire existence becomes working for self-glory. In the end, it is disappointing.

As Christians, our desire should be to use our giftedness to "feel God's pleasure" while we work. This is done as we find ways to let our giftedness be evident in our work. It is common for "worship" leaders to encourage congregations to offer up our best in praise of God. As we work, God is asking the same of us. Whether you find yourself in your vocational sweet-spot, or even if you are in a less than desirable situation, you are still gifted and have oppportunity. Acknowledging your skills as an endowment from God and then being intentional about employing that giftedness to the best of our ability—to *feel God's pleasure*—makes work a form of worship.

Employing Giftedness as an Act of Stewardship

Oxford economist and Christian Donald Hay has suggested that creation gave humans three primary elements: humans are personal, humans are stewards of creation, and humans

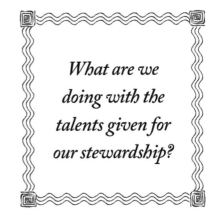

What are we doing with the talents given for our stewardship?

exercise their stewardship through work. Hay reminds us that our gifts have a purpose. Yes, we are to enjoy them and employ them, but ultimately they are resources that we are to *steward*. In biblical terms, to be a steward (*oikonomos*) is to be a manager, not an owner. God is the owner and we are the administrators. Given this basic truth, we offer three primary considerations related to being a faithful Christian steward.

First, to demonstrate stewardship is to work. Hay writes, "Work is the means of exercising stewardship. Mankind is given resources with which to work, *and* he [she] is given the dominion over those resources."[2] In the parable of the talents (Matt. 25:14-30), each person is given a sum of money to be stewarded. The servants receiving five talents and two talents put the money to work. Because they *activated* their gift, they rightfully received praise from their master upon his return. The servant receiving just one talent, however, buried it in the ground. The master condemns him, takes away the talent, and banishes him to outer darkness: "And throw that worthless servant outside, into the darkness, where there will be weeping and gnashing of teeth" (v. 30).

Upon reading this story, many conclude that the master was a shrewd and heartless businessman upset that the "lazy" servant did not make him more money. To read the passage this way, however, would be to miss an important point. The resource put under the stewardship of the third servant was squandered. There is a connection between the biblical idea of talent (which was a sum of money) and our idea of talent today (natural giftedness).

Thus, we may ask: What are we doing with the talents under our stewardship? How are we putting them to work? How are we activating them? Being a good steward does not mean hoarding and protecting our resources; it means putting them to use in an appropriate way. Hay reminds us that "each person is accountable to God for his stewardship."[3] As New Testament scholar Ben Witherington writes, "There are few things as frustrating to God as wasted abilities."[4]

Second, being a faithful steward means using the gifts and resources under our care *for others*. The Bible makes it very clear that the purpose of our gifts is to serve others: "Each of you should use whatever gift you have received to serve others, as faithful stewards of God's grace in its various forms" (1 Peter 4:10). Furthermore, serving others is not to be disconnected from serving the "master," God, who is our original gift giver—the owner of our resources.

Returning to the parable of the talents, the servants activated the talents not simply for themselves, but for their master. Matthew tells us that they "went away at once and put the money to work" (v. 16). The master had "entrusted his wealth to them" and, upon seeing that they employed it appropriately, they were open to "share in the master's happiness" (v. 23).

This is why Jesus talks about letting our light shine—showing off our good works unto others—so that it ultimately points back to God, the gift-giver (Matt. 5:16). Paul Achtemeier helpfully summarizes this understanding of stewardship, with priority to others and to the creator:

> At the end-time throne scene…there is basically one standard of judgment. It is not whether one claims faith or possesses status as a leader in the community of God's people, or one's prophetic or other charismatic abilities. In a way fully consonant with the close of the Sermon on the Mount (especially Matt. 7:21-27), Jesus proposes that the standard of judgment will be whether persons have exhibited in their lives, especially with respect to the least, the lost, and the left out, *obedience to the will of God*.[5]

Further, recall that the talents were entrusted to the servants "according to their ability." Thus, it is not simply a matter of performance, but it is using what is within one's steward-ship in a faithful way—large or small. Whether it is a simple drum or millions of dollars (what five talents is estimated to be worth today), to be a faithful steward is to positively impact others in a way that is glorifying to God. It is not simply about using those gifts at our disposal, but using them efficiently for others to God's glory.

Third, being a faithful steward means serving out of hope and reverence, not fear. One cannot read the parable of the talents without attention to the larger context at the time. Jesus was approaching the end of his ministry and was investing time in teaching his disciples. In addition to the parable of the talents in Matthew's Gospel, Jesus teaches a message of hope, "and they will see 'the Son of Man coming on the clouds of heaven' with power and great glory" (Matt. 24:30).

What is the appropriate response to this hope? For disciples of Jesus, it is careful preparation and an acute sense of readiness, as described through several metaphors and stories such as the fig tree (vv. 32-35), keeping watch (vv. 36-44), the faithful and unfaithful slave (vv. 45-51), and the parable of the ten bridesmaids in Matthew 25. To know Jesus is to know that something very important lies just ahead. This something gives all work for Jesus depth and urgency.

Hope, reverence, and gratitude for our Master inspire activity. Fear, on the other hand, can lead to paralysis. Recall the servant in the parable of the talents who had received one talent and buried it in the ground. How does he justify this action upon the master's return? He pleads, "Master, I knew that you are a hard man, harvesting where you have not sown and gathering where you have not scattered seed. *So I was afraid and went out and hid your gold in the ground*" (vv. 24-25).

The exchange between the unfaithful servant and the master has little to do with risk-taking. Rather, the servant was admonished—"you wicked, lazy servant"—because he did not consider the master's return or interests. "So you knew that I harvest where I have not sown and gather where I have not scattered seed? Well then, you should have put my money on deposit with the bankers, so that when I returned I would have received it back with interest." In other words, the man received his gift and employed it without consideration for the gift giver. He demonstrated a spirit of fear—not faithfulness. He did nothing but wait awkwardly and uselessly. Instead of looking and living in active hope, he looked down and froze in an inactive fear.

To summarize, we all have been blessed with giftedness. To be holy in our work is to respond appropriately to our gifts. We are to both enjoy and employ these gifts. However, to employ them is not to simply use them, but to use

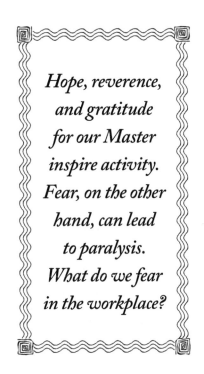

Hope, reverence, and gratitude for our Master inspire activity. Fear, on the other hand, can lead to paralysis. What do we fear in the workplace?

them for a purpose. We manage these gifts, we do not own them: we are stewards. The faithful way to use these gifts is to activate our attributes through work, to use them in ways that assist others and ultimately glorify the Creator, and do this out of a sense of reverence, hope, and anticipation (not fear).

In short, our giftedness is to be a catalyst. Therefore, "in the economic sphere, to ground human action in God's action is to recognize that humankind takes resources divinely provided to use for purposes divinely ordained, and responds properly to the divine call only by consciously acting as steward."[6] As you work as a good Christian steward, your work multiplies the redeeming activity of God's kingdom until Christ returns.

Personalize It

God has done a work in each of us. It is important to realize that God is still at work, still creating. Are you ready to go to work and let your giftedness be a catalyst for God's work? Three ideas have been presented in this chapter related to being a "catalyst."

First, understand that your giftedness is from God and try to explore and embrace who you have been created to be. Second, in the work setting in which you are currently planted, how can you appropriately use your giftedness for God's pleasure? Finally, are you recognizing that by employing your giftedness you are being a good steward of God's creation? Good stewards are divine agents for accomplishing God's will in this world!

We are not suggesting that any of this is easy. Often, we want a simple and quick formula for success, but there is none. You cannot do 1, 2, and 3 and then automatically be a successful catalyst, engaging in your work as worship to God's glory. What is called for is not secret formula or self-help book, but a paradigm shift, a change in life attitude. Two stories illustrate this needed change.

In a recent conversation, I learned of an older Christian who had lost his professional job unjustly and was unable to find another suitable job. Out of necessity for employment, he had become a retail worker in a department store. While there is nothing wrong with being a retail worker, it is not what this person envisioned for his final years of employment given his skills and experience. As we discussed the idea of Work *as* Worship, he remarked that this was now his entire focus. In other words, he was trying to be intentional in discovering how his gifts could be used by God in the setting in which he found himself.

This man, a gifted administrator, now finds himself checking out customers in a department store. He has embraced the possibility that his giftedness has meaning even in his new and unwanted situation. He can intentionally and prayerfully focus the best of his giftedness on being a steward of what God has given him. He had never thought of it this way, but when he works, he is determined to be really worshipping.

The second conversation was with a faculty colleague. This friend said that over twenty years ago, on the day he received his letter conferring on him tenure (meaning that he had job security), he decided to pursue a doctoral degree. Officially, he did not have to. He could have continued to do his job and get the paycheck. But, as a Christian, he realized that he had an obligation to continue to grow and find ways to apply his giftedness to his work, even though it called for significant and unnecessary short-term challenge.

As he reflected on the last twenty years, he expressed his pleasure that he saw his Work *as* Worship and was pleased to have offered his best to God. In those twenty years, this person has led an important academic program that has greatly impacted both Christian and secular higher education. If he had not made the decision to continue to develop and apply his giftedness, this would not have been possible.

We all have a decision to make every day. Are we going to work only to make a living? Or do we see each day as an opportunity to employ our giftedness as a steward of God, to be a catalyst for his works? This attitude, this perspective, this conscious decision reflects a commitment to Work *as* Worship.

What does Work *as* Worship, using your giftedness as a catalyst for God's activity, look like for you, mean to you in your present work setting?

Reflect for Yourself or for Discussion with Others

1. What is your giftedness? What makes you "you" as God's creation?

2. What brings you joy and fulfillment in the workplace?

3. What steals your joy and fulfillment in the workplace?

4. Where do you have the opportunity and freedom in your job to maximize your giftedness?

5. What steps can you take to make your work a responsible act of stewardship?

ENDNOTES

1 Ace Collins, *Stories behind the Greatest Hits of Christmas* (Grand Rapids, MI: Zondervan, 2010).

2 Donald A. Hay. *Economics Today: A Christian Critique*. Grand Rapids, MI: Eerdmans, 1989, 74.

3 Ibid., 73.

4 Ben Witherington, *The Gospel of Mark: A Sociohistorical Commentary* (Grand Rapids: Eerdmas, 2001), 352.

5 Paul Achtemeier, Joel Green, and Marianne Thompson. *Introducing the New Testament: Its Literature and Theology* (Grand Rapids, MI: W. B. Eerdmans Pub., 2001), 115.

6 David J. Atkinson et al, (1995), 115.

CHAPTER 4

Creating Community

*Being "whole" involves intentionally creating
a redemptive community.*

We all want to belong. To find a place and a people who make us feel as though we are part of a community is special. Knowing that these are *my* people and this is *my* place is very special. Sharing life with those closest to us is uplifting and fun. These are the people who are there for us. They are the people who "have your back." Belonging matters.

Is your work a place where you have a strong sense of belonging? For some it may be easy to say "yes." In other cases, that may be the last place you think of as your *community*. Instead, it may be your church, your neighborhood, and/or your family. However, work is how most of us spend the majority of our waking hours. Idealistically, our work environment could be a place where we share an important purpose with others and enjoy being a part of the common venture.

Whether this is your reality or not, this chapter presents the thought that you can be worshiping at work by intentionally creating a sense of "community" or belonging. It explores how the creation of community is one of the Christian's contributions to the workplace.

We already know that community can be formed from the workplace. The tradition of co-workers going out to fellowship at bars and clubs after work is long-standing. Historically, that is where many followers of Christ have separated themselves from the rest of the work community. The issue is not whether we should or should not accompany our work friends to places of fellowship after hours. Our focus is on how our work can be an act of worship as we are intentional about building community among co-workers.

How can we be "salt and light" in the workplace by loving others? By answering this question, our aim is to create a healthy and productive community of believers and unbelievers. Three suggestions are offered. Be reminded that we are suggesting a change in mind-set or attitude (Romans 12:2) and not necessarily offering a step by step formula for how you can make work a worship experience.

The "how" to do it may change from setting to setting, but the attitude stays remains constant.

What is Community?

Picture this as your workday. After entering your office, building, schoolroom, or workshop, you meet with your co-workers in a circle and engage in a relaxed and conversational moment together. This involves story-telling, jokes, and the sharing of notable life events. After this, you plan out the workday and the goals to be achieved as a group. Upon mutual agreement of the day's initiatives, you huddle together and lock arms in a symbolic gesture of unity and then disperse so that you can work diligently and collectively throughout the day. After encouraging, partnering, and assisting each other, you end the day with a guitar sing-a-long, followed by an impromptu appreciation ceremony where your co-workers offer mutual expressions of gratitude for each team-member and recognize each individual's contribution.

Does this sound like your common workday? Of course not. Notions of "community" tend to be romanticized in a way that is unrealistic for the majority of people, making it hard to connect to the idea itself. Indeed, "community" may seem like a distant fantasy in a world of deadlines, hiring and firing decisions, competition, late hours, monotonous activity, angry customers or even angry co-workers, performance evaluations, and constant comparisons between employees.

So what is community? We define community in the workplace as bonding between co-workers where relationships, shared meanings, and a sense of common good is cultivated from a diversity of backgrounds and roles. A sense of belonging comes out of community when I am loved and accepted.

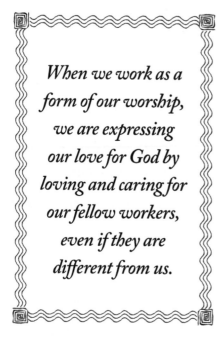

When we work as a form of our worship, we are expressing our love for God by loving and caring for our fellow workers, even if they are different from us.

When we worship, we are expressing our love for God. When we work as a form of worship, we are expressing our love for God by loving and caring for our fellow workers, even if they are different from us. To do so is an act of grace, the way of holiness in action.

Why Does Community Matter to God?

Community is important to God because God is communal by nature and created us to be relational beings. Indeed, God is *triune*, existing eternally as the community of Father, Son, and Holy Spirit.

Recall from chapter two that in answering the philosophical question "Why did God create an earth and a people to inhabit that earth?" we suggested that a better question is, "What does God's choosing to create this tell us about the nature and character of God?" It reveals to us that God is creative—that is, it is in God's very nature to *create* and *relate*. The very reason for creating humans was relational. The entire Bible is the story of God relating to humankind, and the ultimate act of Jesus was to make it possible for us to have a redeemed relationship with God and with others.

Thus, in returning to the question "Why does God desire community?" we may appropriately say that God *is* community, possesses a communal nature, and desires relationships with the creation. If we are image-bearers of a creative and relational God, we participate in the nature of God and honor God when we also create and relate lovingly. To create and love is to be Christ-like, to be holy.

When we use the term "community" we can begin within the church by assessing God's vision for communal worship. Consider a central passage that calls for a "renewal of our mind." Paul's writes: "Therefore, I urge you, brothers and sisters, in view of God's mercy, to offer your bodies as a living sacrifice, holy and pleasing to God—this is your true and proper worship" (Rom. 1:12). Interestingly, the word "bodies" here is *somata* which is plural. And what are these "bodies" to do? They are to present themselves as a living sacrifice, where sacrifice is *thysian*—which is singular.[1]

This reading may strike some as odd. Would it not make more sense if it read: "Present yourselves as living *sacrifices*..."? However, God's desire is not for each person to make an individual sacrifice as they see fit in their own eyes. Rather, God's desire is for his people to make a collective, singular sacrifice. Moreover, this expression, this act of *worship*, makes the most sense if you understand yourself as bound up in a community of faith at worship.

Community matters to God because it is his nature to relate. God created humans so that they would not be alone.

God seeks a relationship with his creation, and his church is designed as "the body of Christ." Relating as a body is in our nature, and even the secular world knows it.

Community matters to God because it is his nature to relate.

We all want to be in a place "where everyone knows our name." It is natural for us to want to be known and belong. It should be natural for a Christian believer to be a grateful and contributing member of the one body of Christ.

The Current State of Community and Work

Any institution—whether it be a business, corporation, department, school, government agency, whatever, requires that the individuals working for that group partner *together* in order to achieve common ends. Thus, community, partnerships, and collaboration are all a natural overflow in the work settings we find ourselves in today.

But is this changing? Trends in the labor force suggest, at least on the surface, that community may not be as natural as it once was. At the same time, the advent of social media is an act of community-building without walls. Technological advances have created an abundance of opportunities to work remotely, being independent of a physical and communal work setting and not in proximity to co-workers.

For example, *Internships.com* lists over 8,000 positions that are virtual by nature—a 20% increase from 2012. Further, a recent survey found that one out of three employers plan to offer virtual internships in the coming year.[2] Consider a recent census poll which found that over thirteen million laborers (approximately 9.4% of the workforce) work at least one day per week from home.[3] However, not all companies are moving in this direction, as evidenced by recent announcements from Yahoo and Best Buy requiring workers to be "in the office" and not to do their work remotely.[4]

Is a virtual workplace a good thing? It depends on how you define "good." Consider an experiment done by the Chinese company *Ctrip*. In response to the rising costs of doing business, the company randomly separated 500 of its employees: half would come to work while the other half would work from home. The results? They found that the group working from home was 13% more productive than the group chosen to work in the office.[5] But the study also found that two-thirds of the original volunteers who wanted to attempt working from their homes later changed their minds and decided to stay in the office. One of the key reasons was "the loneliness of home working."[6]

While it may seem that our physical proximity is a diminishing requirement for achieving real relationships in an age of cyber-technology and its various means for human interaction, there is evidence to suggest that proximity may be more important than we might think. There is an inherent need for us humans to be together.

Robert Putnam of Harvard has challenged the growing belief that proximity is not necessary to achieve community. He refers to computer-based communication as a "shortcut to civic expression" and points to an array of challenges to "the hope that computer-mediated communication will breed new and improved communities."[7] In contrast, he suggests that social capital is a pre-requisite for, as opposed to a consequence of, effective cyber communication.[8] Here is a helpful summary: "Frequent contact on the Internet is a complement to frequent face-to-face contact, not a substitute for it."[9]

Our point is that, whether work is virtual (working from home) or physical (working at the office), engagement, collective partnering, and communal efforts matter. Trends come and go, but community is a part of who we are. Whether your work is on location or remote, you will be interacting with people. How can you discover, and help others discover, a place of community—of true belonging in your work circumstance? The balance of this chapter aims to answer this question.

New Attitudes and Reactions

Looking at yourself, are you always the person that you want to be? Many struggle to be the person they desire to be in Christ. C. S. Lewis put it this way: "There is someone I love, even though I don't approve of what he does. There is someone I accept, though some of thoughts and actions revolt me. There is someone I forgive, though he hurts the people I love the most. That person is me."[10] We are all in need of grace. That is the foundational message of our faith and why Jesus came to earth, died, and was resurrected. God's grace is sufficient for our many needs.

Apply this wonderful message of grace in the workplace where it is very likely that many co-workers will not share our faith in Jesus Christ, our life-style commitments, and maybe our positions on the hot social issues of the day. If we want them to be gracious to us, even though they do not share our commitments, do we not need to show grace to them in spite of our differences and disagreements? Leonard Sweet refers to the C. S. Lewis quote above and asks, "might this be what Jesus means when he commands us to 'love your neighbor as yourself'? Can we extend this level of grace to others, especially those of whom we disapprove?"[11]

Too often in the past Christians have thought that they have a duty to evangelize by telling people "they are going to hell if they do not believe." Without denying this, we invite the reader to consider communicating unconditional love, care, and grace rather than quick and harsh judgments. We are not suggesting condoning or participating in inappropriate behaviors or accepting divergent beliefs that we feel are clearly unbiblical. But we are suggesting that we be intentional about loving and caring for others and not withdraw from people who do not share our views. Instead of starting with the premise that "they are sinners" and that they need to repent, maybe we should consider them as creations of God and engage them gently, much like Jesus did.

Jesus built community and offered grace to people who did not fit into the right religious crowd. He talked to the wrong people. He touched the untouchables. He went to the homes of the hated. He broke the rules about what you can and cannot do on the Sabbath. Jesus often chose acts of grace over acts of condemnation or legalism. Yes, there were times when he needed to express condemnation for not repenting (ironically, expressed most often to the "religious leaders"). But people were drawn to him by his compassion, grace, and mercy. In the end, his crucifixion was the ultimate extension of grace to people who did not deserve it.

So what does this have to do with your work? Work relationships can be healthy and enjoyable. However, in reality, many work settings can be described as rather unpleasant environments, making relationship-building a difficult task. One might be cynical when thinking about notions of grace and community being implemented in a tense, competitive, or relationally shallow work environment. Fortunately, Christians are primed in many ways to address these arrangements. The Christian church, according to the New Testament, is to be a community of faith that breaks down barriers between people.

More importantly, a willingness to break down barriers between people is key. It hinges on the Christian virtues of grace, love, and forgiveness. The community potential in any workplace rides on increasing relationships among human beings and between human beings and God. When we understand that we are relational people and that God has sought us out with unmerited love, we are freed to love others as God loves us. We can love because God first loved us when we were yet sinners and wholly undeserving.

> *Instead of starting with the premise that our co-workers "are sinners" and need to repent, maybe we should consider them as creations of God and engage them gently, much like Jesus did.*

Grace, as we have described it, is not a common notion in the typical work setting. What may be more familiar to us where we work are the concepts of merit and reciprocity, not grace. Merit is the idea of getting only what we have demonstrated that we deserve. If a student does poorly on a test, they merit a poor grade. If a basketball player makes a layup, they merit two points on the scoreboard. Merit for the most part undergirds our judicial system (retribution) and our economic system (distribution). Merit can be good—we need only imagine a chaotic world with no consideration of merit. However, if all considerations related to merit exclusively, then Christians—in addition to everyone else—would be subject to exclusion from God's kingdom: "For all have sinned and fall short of the glory of God" (Rom. 3:23).

It is against this common social pattern of merit that God has chosen to give us an "unmerited" gift of grace. All humankind deserves or merits the sentence of death. And yet, God has given us the gift of grace: "For by grace you have been saved through faith, and this is not your own doing; it is the gift of God—not the result of works, so that no one may boast" (Eph. 2:8-9).

Unfortunately, many stop here. We accept God's grace for us and go about our daily lives. However, in the book of Romans Paul gives us a picture of the purpose of grace. Writing to an audience of people who seemed content to pass judgment on others (without using the same standard of judgment on themselves), he writes: "So when you, a mere human being, pass judgment on them and yet do the same things, do you think you will escape God's judgment? Or do you show contempt for the riches of his kindness, forbearance and patience, not realizing that God's kindness is intended to lead you to repentance?" (Rom. 2: 3-4).

God's grace, an act of unmerited kindness, forbearance, and patience, is intentional. It is intended to lead us to repentance. Receiving this gift is meant to transform us altogether, to make us different people. God's grace brings "salvation to all" and "teaches us to say 'No' to ungodliness and worldly passions, and to live self-controlled, upright and godly lives in this present age" (Titus 2:11-12). In other words, the gift of grace not only changes our eternal trajectory, but it changes us and how we act in this present age. God does not merely want us to receive grace, but desires that we embrace it and endeavor to be "good stewards of the grace of God" through service to one another (1 Pet. 4:9-10).

The other common community principle in the workplace is *reciprocity*. The Latin root of this word means to "return"—i.e., to return one favor for another. To be sure, communities can exist—and exist well—with reciprocity or mutual dependence between its members. Reciprocal relationships define work arrangements, teams, marriages, and even interactions with strangers (since you held this door for me, I will hold the next door for you). However much we can say about reciprocity and its relational importance, it is important to note that it is not the highest relational ideal. In other words, we are not drawn into community simply for the sake of reciprocity, tit-for-tat.

As people of faith, Christians believe that God has extended grace to all, and in turn we are to engage others with a similar form of charity, benevolence, and hospitality. For this reason, Richard Longenecker claims that grace is the "pattern for social morality among God's people."[12] In a work setting, this means engaging co-workers not simply out of reciprocity, where my favor toward them has a boomerang effect of favor back toward me. The engagement is to be solely for their benefit alone. Ultimately, we need to accept co-workers so that they are more likely to feel like they are of value and belong. We need to move beyond reciprocity if our work communities are to be healthy—even redemptive.

We should love our co-workers because Christ loved us and loves them. Further, we may be called on to deliberately reach out to others even if they may have wronged us. Note the important instruction found in 1 Peter 3:9. One way to be holy in the workplace is not repaying evil for evil or abuse for abuse. On the contrary, "repay with a blessing. It is for this that you were called—that you might inherit a blessing." When we love people in this way, they are more likely to feel that they have found a place where they can fit in. We do not do it with the expectation that they will come to church with us or become a Christian (although we will rejoice if this happens). By showing grace to others, we build a community that honors God by enriching the people in the workplace.

A warning needs to be offered. By espousing grace relationships we are not condoning inefficiency, poor behavior, laziness and sloth, or wrong religious beliefs. Nor are we suggesting that we should let people get away with inappropriate actions or be coddled and over-protected. Grace can be abused. But we are suggesting that the attitude of grace, in small acts of kindness, can help break down barriers between people and foster a spirit of community in the workplace.

With these thoughts in mind, we offer three suggestions for building community in the workplace. The goal is to invite others into belonging and hopefully being welcomed into belonging ourselves. Since we all want this, even long for it, how can the Christian at work help to foster community?

1. Clarify for yourself "who I am." The first way to make work worship through acts of creating community is to start with oneself. Moses asked the "Who am I" question in Exodus 3. God's answer to this question was to be found in relationship. The answer was not an explanation of who Moses was in and of himself, but a granting of amazing assurance. Here is who Moses was. He was a called man, called by God, and God would always go with him into his sometimes difficult mission. He would never be a man on his own.

Ask yourself, "Who am I?" More importantly, how do I know who I am? This sounds quite philosophical, right? But at the start of community building we must decide if we are "in" or "out." Do we believe in being relational? Some of you may suggest that, in order to answer the "Who am I?" question, you will need to do self-appraisal to figure yourself out. Obviously, we are not opposed to this. We even suggested in chapter three that you do this when trying to discover your giftedness. But, if you start from an "I" perspective in building community, there may be a lack of awareness of God's perspective on your identity.

Consider an alternative view. The "who I am" should be understood in relation to "whose I am." Yes, this suggests a relationship with Christ. It also calls for us to be in relationship with others. The "whose" is Christ, but it also is the other people who are in your life. Yes, your identity is bound up in part with your church friends, your family, and those people with whom you work. Part of our identity extends beyond "I" to the "we" who are part of our lives. Individuals experience themselves only by means of reflection in a social context. Being an individual requires the presence, not the absence of others. To live is to relate, and to relate is to better understand who I am. It may take two or more of us to know one of us.

Do you walk into work with the attitude, "I am going to do my job and leave everyone else alone?" If so, reconsider it. If you take seriously Work *as* Worship, then embrace the reality that work is an opportunity to belong and to help others belong. Embracing this crucial truth means that you must be open to building relationships, even friendships with people at work, and even if they do not believe as you believe.

2. Identify the common cause at work. After you embrace the relational opportunities at work, look for a common cause to work toward alongside others. We recognize that not every form of community is a godly community. We understand that not every group is a holy network of people. Like any other attribute of the kingdom of God, community has the potential of being distorted or marred by sin. But in a work setting there normally is a common goal.

The purpose of the organization provides a common cause and normally it is in everyone's best interest to work toward achieving this end. Every organizational environment has a purpose by which it mobilizes various resources in order to achieve that purpose. Thus, mission and vision statements, statements of purpose, work environments, or one's organizational culture all serve as efforts to bring resources together for a common purpose.

Whether the goal is to bring fresh water to a third-world village, serve the health needs of a community, run a faithful church, retail a clothing line, or educate kindergartners, these efforts require employees to collaborate in various ways in order to achieve their organization's ends. As a Christ-follower at work, it is an act of worship to define what it is that this group of people at work share in common. It is when you "own" your responsibility to fully engage in this common mission that you begin to let your work be an act of worship. It becomes "as to God" and gives you an opportunity to see others in the workplace, whether they are Christian or not, as your co-laborers. You have something important in common.

3. Become intentional about building relationships. Our third point is that taking on a relational perspective at work means being intentional about developing relationships with co-workers. So far it is established that we need (1) to accept our role in the workplace to love others and (2) to see our workplaces as collaborative relationships with others in order to achieve common ends. An organization may engineer a relationship between two or more people, but this does not mean that they will achieve *community* as we have defined it. Real relationships are deliberate and intentional. Just as we might expect a stark difference between an arranged marriage and a marriage freely and willingly chosen, we must deliberately choose to love others as a means of creating community in our work environment.

The greatest display of intentionality was God sending his Son, Jesus, to the world. Emmanuel, or "God with us," is not simply an idea that God is close or proximate. Rather, it suggests that God came to us and *participated* in daily fellowship with his people. *The Message* translation puts John 1:14 this way: "The Word became flesh and blood, and moved into the neighborhood." What a beautiful way of envisioning Jesus intentionally becoming part of our lives. He comes to us where we are. That is what we need to do for our co-workers.

Being intentional in a workplace requires looking for the best in others, finding ways to connect with them, and developing healthy (holy) relationships. To engender community at work is to see co-workers as image-bearers of Christ, even if they have not accepted God's grace for the forgiveness of their sins. It is important to remind ourselves that our co-workers—those we find ourselves collaborating with to achieve common ends—are not simply people who fill positions (secretary, middleman, janitor, dean). Rather, they are human beings who are loved by God and formed in his image.

Personalize It

As you enter into the community you call work, consider these three thoughts. One, define for yourself "whose I am" and accept your opportunities to build relationships with others in the workplace. Second, identify the common cause in your workplace that brings unity in effort between diverse people. Finally, become intentional about building positive relationships with others in the workplace. Do not see them as a competitor to be bested or a "convert to be won." See them as human beings whom God loves. Let efforts be focused on loving others and let God do his work—in part through you.

We recognize that work situations vary greatly and that this concept of community may seem like a stretch to you. Most people are not blessed to work in a place that reflects Christian values and where actions of grace are common. As your writers, we are very thankful to work in such a place. While it is not a perfect place and there are conflicts from time to time, generally it is a wonderful place to be. Even when there are disagreements, we can still go to lunch together and enjoy each other's company. We care and build together.

This type of workplace may be foreign to you. If so, your attitude is important. On the surface, it is easy to view co-workers as competition, sources of frustration, or barriers to organizational efficiency. However, how might our perspective change when we understand that they are loved by God, that Jesus died for them just as he did for us, and that they carry the image of God even if we have trouble seeing it much of the time?

Going to work with this perspective makes a difference. If you have this attitude, with grace as your tool and the Holy

Spirit by your side, the likely result will be the creation of community. It may not extend to everyone, so have realistic expectations. Small acts, such as expressing appreciation, offering help, buying coffee for someone, or sending a card when a co-worker loses a loved one, can make a big difference. Our suggestions are practical.

Acts of kindness, expecting nothing in return, are like cups of cool water from Jesus. The biggest challenge is how we act or react to people we do not get along with or people who have ill-will towards us. Jesus tells us to "turn the other cheek" and not retaliate, gossip, or undermine another person. These are simple and practical acts that reflect grace.

When there are relational challenges at work, there is a natural tendency to pray, "Lord change them." But the better prayer is, "Lord change *me*." Allow a personal testimony. Years ago while struggling with various workplace challenges that led to compromise and bitterness, this lesson and the corresponding prayer brought about a transformation. After reading "Lord, change me," we all should know that we need to pray this prayer and allow God to change our attitudes and ways.

What happened? Initially, God did not change the challenging people or the situation. God needed to change my attitudes and make me willing to be relational in the workplace. I realized that I had been isolating myself from others in the workplace and I had separated myself from that community, making me "the Christian" in their eyes. I became the butt of jokes. My attitudes had to change and I finally accepted the need to see the workplace as a community-creating opportunity, painful as that might be.

Over time, my focus started to change away from the "issues" and to what we had in common. We were there day after day to serve our customers and help the company be profitable. Each person had a role and I needed to recognize my co-workers as partners, not adversaries or "sinners." Something neat happened. I started liking those people. We had fun setting goals and making good things happened. Over time, friendships formed. I started to get invited to coffee and then lunch. Later, we even met outside the workplace for events.

When my co-workers were in the hospital, I went to see them. When they were sick, I sent get-well cards. They began to reciprocate with acts of kindness. Eventually they inquired about my faith and even asked me to pray for them when they were in challenging situations. When the time came to move on to another job, this group surprised me with a generous gift. I stayed in contact with them for years and found out that a couple of them finally became Christians. I do not know if I had anything to do with that, but I do know that when I left, we were friends and they knew that I loved God and them.

In those years we had many conversations about our views on the news, moral issues of the day, on what behaviors we thought were appropriate or inappropriate. They did not use language that I was comfortable with and did not share my life-style commitments. At times, they seemed to go out of their way to see if they could push my hot buttons and entice me to push them away.

A lesson that was learned then seems appropriate for Christians at all times. We do not have to be in agreement on every issue in order to be in fellowship. In this situation, community was formed and acts of grace were given, back and forth, even though we never came to full agreement on various political, social, or behavioral issues. Yet, we belonged together. I felt like I belonged with them, even with our obvious differences, and they "belonged" with me, even me the "Christian."

What about Where You Work?

We gather at church to worship God. Some in the sanctuary have been Christians for years. Others are just exploring what it may mean to believe in Jesus. As we think of church as the place for worship, we should also see the worship potential in our places of work. When we do, we will be intentional in creating community at work. As we repent from our self-centered nature and embrace our common mission at work, we enter into a collaborative venture. In church we break out in song, celebrating God, and we form supportive communities of faith. In the workplace, let the grace that God offers break out in Work *as* Worship, which may lead to the creation of community, a sense of belonging as and where you work.

Reflect for Yourself or for Discussion with Others

1. Honestly ask yourself, have I accepted my role as the creator of community in my workplace?

2. Who are the people with whom you can naturally connect in the workplace?

3. What can you do to reach out and offer hospitality to them?

4. Who are the people in the workplace with whom you do not connect or with whom you have had conflicts/issues? Have you prayed for them? Have you prayed that God will change you?

5. What can you do to reach out and offer hospitality to the people with whom you do not connect? What are the natural opportunities available for you to express positives to them or to offer yourself to them as a friend?

6. What can you do together, as a team, to have fun and build community? What are the appropriate ways and places within the workplace or outside the workplace for you to build relationships with others without compromising your convictions?

ENDNOTES

1 Richard B. Hays, *The Moral Vision of the New Testament* (Harper Collins, 1996), 35.

2 Jenna Wortham, "Virtually There: Working Remotely," in *New York Times—Education Life*. New York Times, 30 Jan. 2013. Web. Mar. 2013.

3 Neil Shah, "More Americans Working Remotely," in *The Wall Street Journal*. The Wall Street Journal, 6 Mar. 2013. Web. 18 Mar. 2013.

4 For Yahoo, see Julianne Pepitone, "Marissa Mayer Ends Yahoo's Work-from-home Policy." *CNNMoney*. Cable News Network, 25 Feb. 2013. Web. 05 Apr. 2013. For Best Buy, see Pepitone, "Best Buy Ends Work-from-home Program." *CNNMoney*. Cable News Network, 05 Mar. 2013. Web. 05 Apr. 2013.

5 "Can Working from Home Increase Productivity?" *Marketplace—Freakonomics Radio*. American Public Media, 22 Aug. 2012. Web. Mar. 2013.

6 Nicholas Bloom, James Liang, and Zhichun Jenny Ying, "Does Working From Home Work? Evidence from a Chinese Experiment" (Stanford University, 22 Feb. 2013, Web. Mar. 2013, 4.

7 Robert D. Putnam, *Bowling Alone: The Collapse and Revival of American Community* (Simon & Schuster, 2000), 174.

8 Ibid., 177.

9 Wellman, et. al., cited by Putnam, 2000, 179.

10 C. S. Lewis as cited in David Kinnaman and Gabe Lyons, *Unchristian: What a New Generation Really Thinks about Christianity—and Why It Matters* (Grand Rapids, MI: Baker, 2007), 198.

11 Leonard Sweet on *Facebook* (group page). Retrieved March 30, 2013.

12 Richard N. Longenecker, *New Testament Social Ethics for Today* (Grand Rapids, MI: W. B. Eerdmans, 1984), 10.

CHAPTER 5

Contribution

Being "holy and whole" involves
making a contribution.

The last three chapters (Co-creators, Catalyst, and Community) have addressed important paradigm shifts that we believe are necessary to avoid the work-worship divides described in chapter one and to see our work as a form of worship. Worship is a state of being, an essence. It requires a "renewal of the mind" (Rom. 12:2). In Work *as* Worship it is not just about what we *do*; it is about who we *are* and *whose* we are. A faith life that is whole and undivided, holy, will view all activity as glorifying unto God—including our work.

While affirming all of this, let us not dismiss the fact that work also serves a very practical function: *production.* Work is not just about a state of *being*; it also is about a state of *doing.* Although production may elicit thoughts of an assembly line or a manufacturing plant, we use the term in its most basic sense: producing something, creating, building, cultivating, or growing.

Let us gladly embrace the contributions that work can bring. Our work does have a consequence. This could be the production of a product (coffee, house, book, greeting card) or a service (massage, filing taxes, consulting, building a garage, or raising a family). Our work makes a *contribution* to the world we live in.

Can our contribution be a form of worship? Absolutely. This chapter gives attention to how contributing to the particular goal of our workplace can be a worshipful act. We argue that our productive activity can be offered up as an act of worship. We have an opportunity to make the "fruit of our labor" an offering to our God and to embrace the virtue of hard work for a good and noble end.

The Challenge of Scarcity

Scarcity is a reality! To understand why our productive activity is important, we must first understand the pervasive problem of scarcity. Defined and described on the first page on nearly every economics textbook, scarcity is the problem of having infinite desires in a world of finite resources. Or to put it in more general terms, scarcity could be summarized by simply saying that "there isn't enough to go around."

Some of our most contentious societal problems can be traced, in some way or another, back to the problem of scarcity. Specifically, we will look at the problem of justice, production decisions, and social maladies. Each can be an opening to Work *as* Worship.

Justice. Imagine a regular-size pie presented to a group of people for their eating pleasure. If the group is large enough (maybe twenty people), then dividing the pie can become very difficult. Assuming that everyone desires some of the pie, the pie's limited size becomes a problem. Because of this, the group must concern itself with a new set of questions. How much pie should each person get? Should every person even get a piece? How will we decide who deserves the pie?

Now to make the argument even more complicated, replace the word "pie" with "water," "a good education," "clean air," etc. With so many limited resources in our world, the problem of scarcity becomes the problem of justice. To give someone justice means to "render unto them their due" or to give them what they deserve. But here is the problem. How do I determine what someone deserves?

Resolving this question can be difficult and often gets mired in political and philosophical differences. Yet, as Christians, we must care about justice. As Alexander Hill points out, justice is one of the attributes of God and a calling on his people.[1]

Production Decisions. Beyond issues of justice, scarcity is constantly forcing us to determine the best use of our resources. We do it daily in our decision making. At first glance, this may not seem like a problem. However, each of our decisions will inevitably impose a cost. When I make a particular decision about the work I will choose to do, it means I must give up other alternatives. Furthermore, there is a price for giving up an alternative.

For example, suppose a farmer chooses to plant seed corn across his fields in a particular year. By virtue of using the field for seed corn, the farmer has chosen not to plant other crops (beans, wheat, etc.). Nor can he use the field for recreation or any other non-farming use. Why? The answer is that land is *scarce*. There is only so much of it, therefore he must choose to use it in a way that maximizes its potential.

On a larger scale, we see the problem of production decision-making play out all the time. A common example might be choosing between producing wheat and educating children. We could use our land, equipment, and human labor to make more food available across the country, but this means that we could not use these same resources for something else that may be valuable for society (educating children). Conversely, we might educate more children, but we would have less farm production. Or consider income. We could use our money to buy goods and services we want and need today, but this means that we will have less money saved for the future. Or, if we save money for the future, that necessarily means less money that we can spend in the present.

Whatever it is that we may choose, we are forced to forego other alternatives, and this imposes a cost upon us. We might say that scarcity is always *costing* us.

Social Maladies. So far, we have explored how scarcity can create problems in distribution decisions (justice) as well as problems in how we choose to use our time and resources (production decisions). Unfortunately, these problems often create significant outcomes that are negative in nature—e.g., poverty and conflict.

To be clear, eradicating the problem of scarcity would not necessarily remove the problems of poverty and conflict. On some level, people will always be impoverished (emotionally, spiritually, relationally, and morally). Further, history has made clear that conflict is certainly possible even when there is abundance. In other words, humanity's problems extend beyond the issues created by scarcity. There is such a thing as sin.

Poverty is a terribly complex problem that is a reality even in more prosperous countries. Whatever else we might say about poverty, we can say that there are some who have and some who do not have. One author describes it well: "Scarcity limits what we can do. Because of this limit, it is necessary to establish priorities so that we can make decisions. And when we establish priorities, there will always be somebody...that will not be taken care of."[2]

Much has been written over the last decade related to water and scarcity. Approximately 75% of the world's water is used for irrigation, which is important for food production. The other 25% is required for industry and personal use. However, each year the world's population grows by about 80 million people, which is outpacing our current supply of fresh water. The result is increased demand and competition for water across the world.[3]

If the number of people is growing faster than fresh water can be supplied, then persons, villages, or even countries will not have an adequate amount of the water for irrigation, commerce, and personal use. Moreover, water is not simply a luxury item—it is required to lead a healthy, productive life. It is for this reason that the Food and Agricultural Organization (FAO) declared that "water scarcity is an issue of poverty."[4]

In addition to poverty, arrangements where some people have and others do not are a natural recipe for conflict. This line of thinking reaches back a long way. For example, the seventeenth-century political philosopher Thomas Hobbes believed that competition for scarce resources was the primary source of human conflict.[5] It is difficult to disagree with Hobbes. Whether it is children fighting over toys, co-workers competing for a project, our recent "Occupy Wall-Street" demonstrations, or even despite third-world environments, any arrangement where some people's needs are met and the needs of others are not will create tension. There is an abundance of research to support this belief.

To return to the example of water scarcity, one expert suggested that conflicts over water are as old as recorded history.[6] Water aside, shortages have incited aggressive behavior from biblical times to the present. Scarcity creates problems, including poverty, and poverty—or not having enough—is a recipe for human conflict.

Addressing the Problems of Scarcity: Productive Activity

Scarcity will always be present in nearly any environment where we find ourselves. There is one force, however, that can serve to minimize its negative effect. That force is *growth*. Our work activity can make a contribution to growth and development in a way that fends off the threat of scarcity. Scarcity is the problem of not having enough; production is the solution of creating more.

Proverbs 14:4 describes this simple philosophy well: "Where there are no oxen, there is no grain; abundant crops come by the strength of the ox." In other words, when we work we produce and our needs are satisfied. Or as *The Message* translation puts it, "No cattle, no crops." No activity, no output. No work, no growth of supply.

How does our productive activity address the problems of scarcity? Let us return to our pie example where we must split a small pie among 20 people. In this situation, the problem of justice becomes acute. How do we determine who gets some of the pie? How much goes to each? What criteria do we base this decision on?

What if the supply changed? Imagine that we had ten pies as opposed to just one. Now the considerations involved in a just distribution—while still important—tend to lose their sting. There is an ample amount of pie to go around and satisfy the desires of all those present.

According to the World Health Organization, only approximately one-third of the world's population has adequate access to essential life-sustaining medicine and medical treatment opportunities.[7] In poor countries, paying money for access to medicine means giving up an array of other important resources for which the money could have been used, purchasing education, food, shelter, etc. However, medical developments, innovative technologies, and enhanced distribution methods are changing this terrible situation to some extent.

While there is much work to be done, new medical tests and procedures are now available at affordable prices in countries, towns, and villages desperately in need of medical access. One recent example has been provided by Harvard chemist George Whitesides who has created medical diagnosis devices the size of postage stamps at virtually no cost.[8] With growth enhancements such as this, the "costs" of our decisions become lower and lower.

Bloomberg *Businessweek* recently published an article in which a panel of experts was asked how they would address worldwide water supply and management problems. Among other things, they spoke about large-scale "desalination" programs throughout the world (removing salt from ocean water for domestic use), rainwater harvesting systems, lake water extraction, and other alternatives such as fixing leaky water-pipes and shifting consumer psychology--how they think about water usage.[9]

Here is the key point to be made. There are real solutions for addressing the problem of water shortage evident in the world today. Moreover, these solutions require ideas, design, and implementation through the collaboration of people, places, and things. The work being done to address water shortages is productive activity that makes a very real and lasting contribution across the globe. This will help lift many out of places of poverty. Furthermore, it will reduce conflict or the potential for conflict in a multitude of settings.

Increasing the water supply is just one example of growth solving the scarcity problem. In reality, there are thousands upon thousands of examples where productive activity through our work has made a real and lasting contribution. This is good. This is God's work. It is the social holiness of hands at work producing for the benefit of humanity.

What Does This Mean for You and Me?

Here is the bottom line. Growth in available resources occurring from productive activity enhances living standards for individuals and societies across the world. Not only do we grow the supply so that there is more to go around (a larger pie), but we *innovatively grow*. When creative ideas are met with productive determination, not only do we produce more, we actually change the kind of world we and others live in.

Innovative activity increases convenience, enhances existing products and services, and opens new doors not yet imagined. It was innovation that led to the discovery, production, and wide-scale distribution of penicillin, a medicine that could kill the bacteria responsible for life-threatening diseases. It was innovation that created an affordable car—the Model T—through revolutionary production methods. Further, expanded highways and suburbanization, important social movements and landmark legislation, and even the internet are all products of innovative activity.

In the future, innovation will lower our utility costs, create better tools to educate our children, offer new methods by which to communicate with each other, and improve the health and quality of living for millions of people across the globe. Innovation coupled with productive activity can make the world a better, more convenient place.

Unfortunately, sometimes solutions to problems create new problems that have to be resolved. The unending cycle of problems, solutions, and emerging new problems is illustrated in a history lesson provided by John Waters, an innovator in the electronic car industry.

What was one of the primary drivers leading to the internal combustion engine we now use in automobiles? It was an environmental issue. In the late 1800s the presence of an increased population of horses in urban areas was creating a terrible problem. It had consequences not only for the quality of life, but even for the existence of life.[10] Something had to be done. Crisis and innovation led to a solution.

Now, over a hundred years later, the compelling reason to find an alternative to the carbon fuel-burning internal combustion engine is also environmental. With so many automobiles burning oil-based products, we need to find an alternative. Solutions are moving forward. As we transition to new transportation devices, who knows what future problems will call for new innovation.

Our work can be glorifying to God by *co-creating*, being a *catalyst* for God's glory, and engendering *community*. But our work also *contributes* to the world around us through the creation of products and services that improve the lives of others and leave a lasting imprint across the world's landscape. Our faith in God needs to be expressed through practical action in the workplace.

We need to produce. We need to contribute. As Christians, we should be known for this. It should be an outgrowth of God's fruit in our lives. Too often we have heard of outspoken Christians in the workplace who are known for sloth, laziness, and unproductive behavior. This is not reflective of Work *as* Worship. We should be, and probably normally are, known as the "contributors" to our organization's mission.

However, we do not want to end here. Believers may make a contribution through their work, but we also can conceive of our productive activity in a faithful manner. It is not just about production or productivity, but understanding the nature of the contribution that we make. People of faith have an important role to play in this task, which we will explore next.

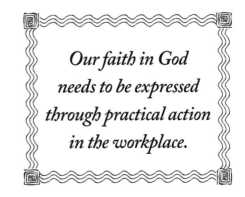

Our faith in God needs to be expressed through practical action in the workplace.

Making Production an Act of Worship

Scarcity creates problems. However, work activity, innovation, production, and growth can ward off the problems that scarcity tends to create. This contribution can be a very visible act of worship. As mentioned, Christians can help others by making their lives easier and more manageable. Our work can make the world a better place, whether from an accountant's desk, an international mission agency, the coach's office, a home, hospital, classroom, workshop, or any other potential work environment. In a word, our work *helps* others.

How can what you do in work and what you contribute through work be an intentional act of worship? How can you conceive of your work and productivity in a more faithful manner? Consider the following three thoughts as possibilities.

Scarcity and God's Abundance. We already have given attention to the problem of scarcity. Productivity and growth can help to offset the sting of scarcity. However, as Christians we must recognize another key attribute to the equation of scarcity: *unlimited desire*. Limited resources are not the only problem. Unlimited desire is equally if not more problematic than the limited resources.

Unlimited desire, or what many call insatiability, means that we will never be satisfied. To think otherwise is to over-estimate fallen human nature. One such miscalculation came from the famous economist John Maynard Keynes in a 1928 speech given at Cambridge University. The address—which was titled "Economic Possibilities for our Grandchildren"—made two predictions Keynes believed would occur one-hundred years from that time.

First, Keynes predicted enormous growth and output per person which would usher in an age of abundance and riches. Second, and related, increases in wealth and income would decrease the amount of hours that we work in society. Specifically, he predicted we would work 15 hours a week per person by 2030.[11]

Today economists agree that Keynes was amazingly accurate in his forecast as it related to output, growth, and technological advancement. However, he missed the mark completely as it related to easing off on work. What was the error? Authors Robert and Edward Skidelsky give a clear statement as to the nature of the miscalculation: "Keynes believed that people had a finite quantity of material needs that might one day be fully satisfied. He believed this because he failed to distinguish wants from needs."[12] If our wants become confused with needs, we will never have enough. This is the problem of desire. We humans are burdened with the problem of unlimited desire—what we often refer to as *greed*.

Desire, and more specifically the "desires of the flesh" (Gal. 5:16-17), are not spoken of highly in the Christian faith tradition. In other words, it is not our desire, per se, that is to be condemned, but the kind of desire we are cultivating within and among ourselves. As Will Willimon explains, "The church is a school of desire, teaching us what things are worth wanting, what desires are worth fulfilling."[13] This sharply contrasts with the pursuit of material items or our desire for more and more "stuff," which can closely be related to idolatry in biblical thought.[14] We need only recall Christ's parable of the seed, where the seed falling among the thorns yields no grain because "the cares of the world, the lure of wealth, and the desire for other things come in and choke the word" (Mk. 4:7-19).

In addition to possessing a more faithful perspective on desire, Christians should also recognize that scarcity is an earthly problem to which God is not subject. Because of this, Christianity will always question the notion of scarcity. In a world marked by limited resources, contention, and despair, we appeal to a God of abundance, cooperation, and hope.

If scarcity is a problem, then our production—our contribution—is a means to address this problem. However, Christians must also recognize that scarcity is just as much a problem of unlimited desire as it is a problem of limited resources. To be a person of faith is to desire appropriately, and to appeal to a God of abundance who "calls his own sheep by name" (Jn. 10:3), knows our needs (Matt. 6:8), and will meet those needs "according to the riches of his glory in Christ Jesus" (Philippians 4:19).

Acknowledge the Limits to Innovation. As stated earlier, productive activity and creative innovation have not only advanced the amount of goods and services per person in modern societies, but also created a more advanced, sophisticated, and convenient world. To provide an example, National Public Radio's business and economics show "Planet Money" once posed the following question: "Would you rather be rich in the year 1900 or middle-class now?" Interestingly, over two-thirds of the respondents chose "middle-class now."[15]

For our purposes, we are less concerned about the "correct" answer to this question. We point rather to this as an example of our extraordinary leaps in innovation. The very fact that one would have to consider such a question is strong evidence of the tremendous amount of productive innovation amassed over the last century. Economist Tim Taylor says that there is a lesson to be learned in the "rich 1900 or middle-class now." question: "The force of economic growth over time has given middle class people in America...things that would have been regarded as miracles a century ago. And having access to those miracles is worth an enormous amount."[16]

As Taylor's quote makes clear, our labor—coupled with creativity and technological ingenuity—makes our innovative progress seem nothing short of miraculous. In spite of this, an important question remains: Is innovative progress the same as moral progress? Innovative activity has made us better cars, phones, medicines, bridges, airplanes—but has it made us better people?

We are not the first to pose these questions. At the close of 2009 and in the wake of the worst financial crisis in the United States since the depression era of the 1930s, the authors writing for *The Economist* took stock of the term "progress" and its contemporary definition. Despite the financial meltdown, one might expect a ready defense of our innovative activity. After all, this is still the most prosperous century on historical record. An historical survey of past periods of economic, scientific and technological prosperity reveals no parallel when compared to our present context, and this alone is reason enough for pause when considering the distribution of blame in the wake of the financial crisis. In short, we may encounter problems, but our growth and innovation is worth the cost.

However, this was not the inevitable conclusion reached in that 2009 article. Indeed, amidst centuries of increased efficiency in producing food, science, industrial growth, technological innovation, and gains in overall wealth among both rich and poor nations, such "material progress" has failed to deliver emotional sat-

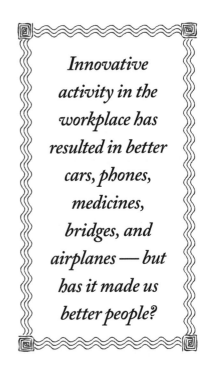

Innovative activity in the workplace has resulted in better cars, phones, medicines, bridges, and airplanes — but has it made us better people?

isfaction, overall happiness, and social solidarity. Rather, the author writes, one of the more visible outcomes of our "prosperity" is the attrition of life around us: "The forests are disappearing; the ice is melting; social bonds are crumbling; privacy is eroding; life is becoming a dismal slog in an ugly world."[17] Citing the philosopher Susan Neiman, the article suggests that our behavior should not be shaped by power, material wealth, etc., but rather by what is "right" despite the inconveniences that accompany the pursuit of this ideal. Moral and not just material development is a more appropriate measurement of progress and prosperity.

Christians should applaud this statement. It is a clear expression of what those in the faith tradition have understood for centuries: the problem is sin. Sin, or its Greek expression of *missing the mark*, is not a problem that can be solved through creative work, productive activity, or technological innovation. It is a spiritual problem. It is a problem, writes Paul, of the *flesh*: "For the flesh desires what is contrary to the Spirit, and the Spirit what is contrary to the flesh. They are in conflict with each other, so that you are not to do whatever you want" (Gal. 5:17).

With this in mind, Christians must continually recognize and communicate the difference between productive activity that allows persons in society to live well and God's life-transforming Spirit who allows a person to live whole. True progress, just as *The Economist* authors recognized, must also account for our change as people in moral and ethical terms—not simply changes in the things we create and consume.

There is a helpful quote attributed to D. L. Moody that captures the gap between moral/spiritual progress and progress of any other sort. He writes: "If a man is stealing nuts and bolts from a railway track, and in order to change him you send him to college, at the end of his education he will steal the whole railway track." Moral progress, as Moody points out, is not a matter of intellect, technology, or the right material resources. It is a matter of the heart. The more we know and we have can lead to a situation in which we do the wrong in a more clever way and on a more massive scale.

> *Christians must continually recognize and communicate the difference between productive activity that allows a person in society to live comfortably and God's life-transforming Spirit who allows a person to live whole.*

Furthermore, progress—whether it is educational, material, or even philosophical—cannot change the nature of a person's heart. When Alfred Lord Tennyson exclaimed, "Oh that a man would arise in me that the man I am would cease to be," or when Mark Twain cynically wrote, "'Be yourself' is about the worst advice you can give to some people," or even when Paul cried out, "Oh wretched man that I am, who will save me from this body of death?" these expressions appealed to a higher power for moral and spiritual advancement; not material progress. In other words, we are perpetually reminded of a need for a savior outside of ourselves.

Individuals across the world can and have participated in making a contribution to society through their work activity. We encourage Christians to do likewise. But people of faith must enhance this understanding of contribution by recognizing and espousing the fact that our moral development and advancement is not merely a matter of production (we do not produce and innovate ourselves into becoming *better* people) but submission to a life-altering relationship with God.

Redeeming Contributions. Several years ago I shared an essay I had written on the environment with a close friend who is a pastor. In it I mentioned the Sierra Club, a group heavily committed to environmental stewardship and protection in the United States. However, when it came to religion and specifically to Christianity, one of the Sierra Club's board members was considerably outspoken about his antagonism toward the

Christian faith and its skewed views of creation and nature. To the modern mind, he wrote, the words of Jesus are nothing more than "grotesque, apocalyptic nonsense."[18] Among other aspects of the paper, I addressed the flawed nature of such thinking, defending—to the best of my ability—the Christian faith perspective as it related to nature and stewardship.

Assuming my friend would return a long email praising my paper, I was surprised by his short response: "So, is the work of the Sierra Club...good?" After thinking through this for some time, I realized his point: the group may have anti-Christian members, but does this make the group's work anti-Christian as well? Can I label environmental stewardship—the protection of God's creation—as something *non-Christian* just because it is undertaken by a person or persons who are not of the faith? Does doing God's work cease to be good when it is done by people who do not set out to honor God?

These questions stand as a reminder that we do not create themes of love, compassion, charity, grace, etc.—these are God's themes. God authored them. Thus, when we act upon these themes, we are participating in a God-authored activity (not one created by us). When work activity is undertaken to help the poor, show compassion for the elderly, nurture and educate children, or protect the environment, it is God's work. Christians should be mindful of this so that they can "take back" these themes—the very definition of the word *redeem*.

When a group such as the Sierra Club does work that is consistent with the things important to God, Christians should see that work as redemptive. In other words, Christians can recognize work activity—whether it is spiritual or secular—as making a kingdom contribution and labeling such activity appropriately.

Having this perspective, imagine the doors this opens for people of faith working in a secular environment. Have you ever seen a movie, heard a song, or watched a show that dealt with the theme of grace or forgiveness? Have you ever come across a non-profit organization whose driving ethos was compassion? What about a school that wants to teach children character and responsibility? Or a medical treatment center whose mission is to heal the ailments—mental, physical, and emotional—of their clients? The point is that these themes (grace, compassion, character-development, healing, etc.) are *God's themes*. They were not authored by secular artists, schools, non-profits or hospitals. They were authored by God. Imagine Christians throughout the world working in these fields and properly redeeming—taking back—these themes under the umbrella of God's desires for humankind.

To steward the environment, help a child learn to share, assist the poor and elderly, or create a device that brings clean drinking water to a third-world village is to make an important contribution. To redeem these acts as God-created and God-sponsored themes is to make an additional contribution to the original service. When the world captures these themes and "answers wisely," we like Jesus can respond: "You are not far from the kingdom of God" (Mk. 12:34).

At the start of this chapter we said that work is not just a state of being. It is also a state of doing. Our faith, attitude, and perspective are important for us to worship God in our work lives. We must not dismiss the fact that our work can make a real and lasting contribution.

The problem of scarcity creates an abundance of problems that we seem to encounter in one form or another on a daily basis. However, the growth and innovation that come from our work activity should help to alleviate the negative social and economic effects of scarcity, thus making a lasting contribution that is both important and beneficial to others.

We wish to end this chapter by stressing one point. People of faith can make an important contribution to their work. How? Christians recognize that the crux of scarcity comes from unlimited desire just as much, if not more, than it does from limited resources. Furthermore, we serve a God who is not subject to scarcity, but whose very nature is one of abundance. Christians also recognize that material progress is not moral progress and that sin is a spiritual problem—not a political, economic, or social problem that can be addressed merely through productive efforts.

Finally, we emphasize again that workers can partner with Christians and non-Christians alike in job efforts that participate in God-authored themes. Whether knowing it or not, many organizations are doing the work of God. Christians can redeem such initiatives under the blanket of kingdom efforts. Recognizing all of this, we submit that to produce is to contribute. This is an act of worship. It is an essential aspect of a holy life.

Personalize It

Work *as* Worship may look like the following as you strive to make a distinctive contribution in your workplace.

First, work hard to accomplish much. Make work an act of worship by giving your all to the task. The primary goal is not to earn a lot or to become successful. It may happen, but the focus is on the love of the work. One of my good Mennonite friends is always talking about doing "good work." By this he means meaningful work that makes a positive contribution to people and society. At the end of the day, we should feel physically spent, yet fulfilled because we did our best work and left something good behind. Be aware of your productivity and consider the essence of what you are doing and the good it produces.

Live a frugal life. Consider keeping your material life relatively simple. Live so that you are contributing to abundance, not scarcity. Do not demand "more" all the time just to sustain your ambition for things. This does not mean that we cannot have some nice things, but consider what is really needed and do not become over committed to unwarranted wants. Set a budget. If your prosperity grows, give more away. At the end of the day, do not let what you have acquired be the measurement of your value. Build community with others while you work and celebrate the beauty of good relationships.

Have you ever been with a group of people working hard together and the group breaks out in song? It is as if they are "worshipping." It reminds me of the times when our church groups have gone on short-term mission trips. During those trips, I have physically worked harder than I ever have. As we worked, we talked, laughed, sang and shared a common commitment to do something meaningful. At the end of the day, exhausted, I felt like I had been part of a team that did something important. It felt good.

See beauty from God in all forms and places, even if it is not explicitly "Christian" or the product of a follower of Christ. Celebrate the good work that is done. Yes, you can do it in God's name, and you can praise God when you see it done by those who do not share your faith. Be about appreciation, praise, encouragement, and celebration.

There may be a temptation to separate ourselves from non-Christians in the workplace. There of course are reasons not to become entangled in inappropriate behaviors, talk, and attitudes. In response, there is a temptation to become isolated as "the Christian" in the workplace. It is true that some faith traditions encourage separating from society—as some wings of Christianity have done. Our advice is to find appropriate ways to "lean in" (a phrase of Sheryl Sandburg).[19] The workplace should be a place where we as Christians are differentiated primarily because our productivity speaks of God's abundance, not by our awkward isolation from others.

Our actions as Christians in the workplace should suggest that our priorities are serving, helping, and sharing, and that this is a praise testimony to our God carried on with and intended to be on behalf of our co-workers. We should be known for our appreciation of the work of others, even if we disagree with them about faith. Let our attitudes and deeds suggest that we respect, value, and love humankind and see God's hand in all the work for good that is done.

Reflect for Yourself or for Discussion with Others

By making a contribution through our work, we are worshipping God. Consider these questions carefully, and very personally.

1. What are ways that you can improve your productivity at work?

2. What have you accomplished at work that makes you feel like it is "good work"?

3. Do you have a financial budget and strive to live by it?

4. What can you live without and still live well?

5. What can you do to make work more fun and enjoyable?

6. What work is being done that you admire and respect, even if it is done by a person who does not share you commitment to Christ?

7. What can you learn from good things done and things done well by others?

ENDNOTES

1 Alexander Hill, *Just Business: Christian Ethics for the Marketplace* (Downers Grove, IL: InterVarsity, 1997), 14.

2 Jung Mo Sung, *Desire, Market and Religion* (London: SCM, 2007), 106.

3 "UN-Water Statistics--Water Resources," *UN-Water Statistics--Water Resources,* United Nations (Water), n.d. Web. 14 Apr. 2013.

4 "FAO Water Unit--Water News: Water Scarcity." *FAO Water Unit--Water News: Water Scarcity.* Food and Agricultural Organization Water Unit, n.d. Web. 14 Apr. 2013.

5 Richard G. Wilkinson, *The Impact of Inequality: How to Make Sick Societies Healthier* (New York: New, 2005), 5.

6 Laurie Goering, "Water Scarcity to Drive Conflict, Hit Food and Energy, Experts Say." *Trust.org.* Alertnet--A Thomson Reuters Foundation Service, 17 Apr. 2012. Web. 14 Apr. 2013.

7 Roger Bate and Richard Tren, "The WTO and Access to Essential Medicines," *The WTO and Access to Essential Medicines.* American Enterprise Institute, 16 Feb. 2006. Web. 22 Apr. 2013.

8 "George Whitesides: A Lab the Size of a Postage Stamp," *TED: Ideas Worth Spreading.* Feb. 2010. Web. 22 Apr. 2013.

9 "How the Experts Would Fix the Water Supply," *Bloomberg Businessweek: Innovation and Design. Bloomberg Businessweek,* 21 Mar. 2013. Web. 15 Apr. 2013.

10 John Waters, then CEO of Bright Automotive and currently with ECHO Automotive, in a speech at the Dickmann Scholarship Luncheon in Anderson, IN, December, 2009.

[11] Robert Skidelsky and Edward Skidelsky, *How Much Is Enough?: Money and the Good Life* (New York: Other, 2012), 69.

[12] Ibid., 25.

[13] William H. Willimon, *Shaped by the Bible* (Nashville: Abingdon, 1990), 80.

[14] Hay, 1989, 71.

[15] "Would You Rather Be Rich in 1900, Or Middle-Class Now?" Planet Money. National Public Radio (NPR), 12 Oct. 2010. Web. 17 Apr. 2013.

[16] Ibid.

[17] "Onwards and Upwards." *The Economist* 19 Dec. 2009: 37-40.

[18] Bernard Zaleha, "Christian Ecology--Recovering Christian Pantheism as the Lost Gospel of Creation," *Christian Ecology--Recovering Christian Pantheism as the Lost Gospel of Creation.* Christian Ecology, 20 Apr. 1997. Web. 16 Apr. 2013.

[19] Sheryl Sandberg and Nell Scovell, *Lean In: Women, Work, and the Will to Lead* (New York: Alfred A. Knopf, 2013).

CHAPTER 6

Conclusion

Let a holy praise ring out where you work!

Think about this. When you go to work, you are given an opportunity by God to worship, witness, and serve. For some, this idea may seem brand new. But is it really new? Actually, we can trace the notion of our work being done as an act of worship back to the Bible. Indeed, the idea of Work *as* Worship is found in the very definition of the word "worship."

A review of the Greek text leads to an interesting discovery. The word for worship actually means acts of service and work. In this sense, worship literally means "to serve or to work." Like so many other words, *latreia* or its verbal form *latreuo* have multiple meanings in classical Greek usage. On the one hand, its non-biblical use refers to work or service as a means to earn wages or for a reward (very similar to our modern notions of work). In its biblical use, however, it refers to service that is offered unto God. Specifically, the Greek verb *latreuo* often refers to serving God in other arenas of our life.

Related to this is the word *leitourgia* which refers to the work of the people. Our contemporary word "liturgy" comes from this particular Greek expression. Liturgy is "human action in response to the religious vision."[1] Thus, *latreia/latreuo* evolves from work as a means to earn a *wage* into its biblical use of work as a means to serve and *worship* God. Returning to Romans 12:1-2, we see this clearly in Paul's use of the term:

> I appeal to you therefore, brothers and sisters, by the mercies of God, to present your bodies as a living sacrifice, holy and acceptable to God, which is your spiritual worship [*latreia*]. Do not be conformed to this world, but be transformed by the renewing of your minds, so that you may discern what is the will of God—what is good and acceptable and perfect.

Here, for Paul, service is not simply meant to garner a wage (for ourselves) but to honor our Creator (God). Literally, our work and our service are meant to be an act of spiritual worship. What is the means to accomplish this? Paul tells us that it is being "transformed by the renewing of our minds."

However, this may not be easy. It will indeed take a "renewing of the mind." As we go to work we step into an entirely new realm where there is a possible conflict between who we say we are and who we really are. Be reminded of the Ketchel story in chapter one. If we are going to "stick to the script" and live a life of integrity, we need to acknowledge the temptation to be divided.

The Identity Arena

Imagine that you are standing in the middle of a large sports arena. You find yourself surrounded by thousands of ticket-holders who you think might have come just to see you perform. However, these are not spectators of you or any team; they are not there to watch you. Rather, they are there to *tell you who you are*. You are in the *Identity Arena*.

Some shout on microphones. Others hold up signs. Others whisper, make subtle gestures, or do something else to draw your attention. They want to tell you what to believe, how to act, why you exist, and where to look for answers. In short, they want to tell you something about who you are or should be. They want to confer an identity upon you.

Sound like a bad dream? So many suggestions and messages communicated in so many ways is an overwhelming thought. Most would not want to find themselves in this intimidating arena. In many ways, however, we all are already there. Marketing experts estimate that on any given day we are confronted with approximately 3,000 to 4,000 impressions (or mini-advertisements). A t-shirt message, a billboard, a radio spot, a television commercial, a logo, or a webpage banner—all are examples of the legion of messages that we encounter daily.

To be clear, many advertisements are informative. They shape our decisions about what we buy in helpful, functional ways. However, other advertisements—in an effort to "recruit consumers"—are used to arouse our emotions.[2] They evoke feelings, sentiments, reflection, anticipation, and individuality. As we entertain these voices, messages, proclamations, we risk creating multiple conceptions about who we are. The result? Too many notions about who we are means that "traditional ideas of identity will be less meaningful."[3] In other words, we will be divided as persons, persons impacted by a selfish marketplace seeking to alter identities to its own ends.

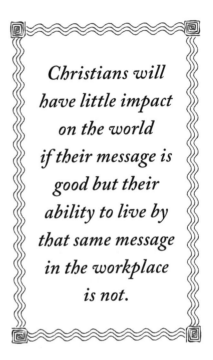

Christians will have little impact on the world if their message is good but their ability to live by that same message in the workplace is not.

One of the primary points we hope to make is that a divided life, an unholy life, is a threat to a faithful expression of our Christianity. A friend, remarking about a loved one, once told me: "I guess the best thing I could say about her is that she was very wise, but she could not live up to the standard of the wisdom she preached." I can recall thinking that such a statement was less of an innocent observation and more of an indictment. Christians will have little impact on the world if their message is good but their ability to live by that same message is not.

The metaphor of the *Identity Arena* is a reminder that, if the wind blows in the direction of multiple identities, we must be resolute in our determination to be whole. We must strive to have integrity in all that we do because it will not occur naturally. Many conflicting winds there surely are, so being *intentionally* whole—holy—is a must!

Living Whole in the Work/Worship Divides

With all the pressure to be different things to different people in different places, the pressure of the Identity Arena is real. In this book, we have sought to give attention to consistency between our faith life and our work life. In chapter one we discussed four common "divides" to which Christians can easily fall prey.

The first divide, Work *not* Worship, is when our Sunday-self is different from our Monday-self. I may feel, speak, and behave faithfully in the right spiritual venue, but I take on a different persona in a more non-spiritual venue—like a workplace. For example, Camp writes: "'He's really a very serious Christian,' someone once told me about a very high-profile businessman in Nashville, 'but you just wouldn't know it by the way he practices business.'" This leads Camp to conclude: "The disjunction between the 'church' and the 'secular' continues to reign in much Christian practice."[4]

In honest moments, the Christian in this divide will probably admit that this is not right and find ways of justifying this disjunction or attempt to give penitence for it by donating money from the fruit of their work. It is not uncommon to hear successful people who are Christians say that they wanted to be as successful as possible so that they can give as much as possible, as if that justifies the divide.

A second common mistake is the Work *then* Worship divide. Here, we desire to exercise our Christianity in other areas of our life (e.g., our jobs), but our faith plays "second fiddle" to those job characteristics and priorities. Unfortunately, under this paradigm our faith merely fills in the blanks of our regular work lives.

Even worse, many under this divide believe that their faith is a "lucky-charm" that will assist them in success. This dismisses the reality that being faithful may very well be accompanied by hardship, heartache, and marginalization. If being faithful is a recipe for receiving blessings (as many preach today), then we risk making Jesus a formula, not a life-transforming Savior. We worship an idol, not God, when we try to make God a means to an end that conveniently serves our own self-interest. This is far from worship. Creating attributes of God that suit me is, as A. W. Tozer once suggested, the very definition of idolatry.[5]

One's faith identity should redefine, redeem, and restore the whole of life—sanctify it. It should transform who we are inside out, leading to changes in the way we think and act. However, under this divide and among the impoverished conceptions of God it tends to breed, our faith is always tempered—defiled--by alternate pursuits and desires.

The third divide we mention in chapter one is not so much a divide as it is an illegitimate marriage between our faith and work lives. The Work *and* Worship mentality is the act of over-spiritualizing all work-related activity. The good, the bad, and the ugly are all chalked up to "God's intervening hand." Strategic decisions are euphemized as God's will. Three notable problems emerge from this.

First, invoking God's name for an organizational decision makes disagreement rather difficult. If a manager or co-worker remarks, "I believe God wants us to do strategy X," then assessing the merits of this strategy becomes an uncomfortable exercise since you might find yourself disagreeing with "God's will." Second, the inappropriate blending

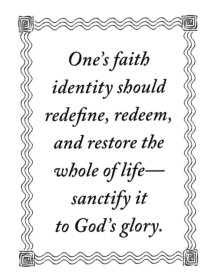

One's faith identity should redefine, redeem, and restore the whole of life— sanctify it to God's glory.

of work and worship leaves little room for the mundane and the ordinary. It is important to relish and celebrate our mountain-top spiritual moments, but—like Jesus himself—we must come down from the mountain. Much of our lives are lived in the valley and we must learn what it means to be faithful in those places.

Finally, this paradigm can naturally lead to exhaustion. Our faith life should energize us, not make us weary. However, exhaustion is precisely what we risk if we believe that our work lives and our spiritual lives are two separate spheres that we must give ourselves to entirely. If we find ourselves facing exhaustion in this divide, how do we become whole? How do we live with integrity? How do we find a holiness relevant to our jobs? How do we reflect a holiness without which no one will see God?

The final divide sets up our faith life and our work lives as an either-or choice: Work *or* Worship. If I am a Christian, then I should work in ministry. If I were to choose otherwise, then I would be compromising opportunities to be faithful. This divide assumes that only church ministry is *ministry*, and that everything else is a "secular" job that requires an entirely different paradigm. While it is certainly true that being a pastor and being an accountant, nurse, or small business owner will require different job functions, we reject the notion that, for a Christian, one is ministry work and the other is not.

> *If we can live our work lives as an act of worship, we are more likely to be living a whole and a more holy life.*

In light of these divides, what are we to do? Instead of thinking of work and worship as different expressions of life, let us try to see them as one. If we can live our work lives as an act of worship, we are likely to be living a more whole, and we suggest a more holy life. Such a life, one of integrity, is highly desirable.

Cultivating Wholeness and Integrity

To combat the problems created under the work-worship divides, we have provided an alternate paradigm: Work *as* Worship. To support this, we offered the 4 C's that comprise this paradigm: *Co-creating* with God, being a *Catalyst* for God's work through our gifts, engendering *Community* in our places of work, and making a lasting and faithful *Contribution* in and through the environments that we work within.

We believe that to be holy involves being consistent and whole in all aspects of our lives, and this includes our work lives. To live otherwise is to live divided. However, achieving wholeness is not as easy as we may think. Here, are two primary reasons why this is so.

First, as we sought to make clear earlier in the chapter, we live in a world with an array of voices competing for our attention. We live in the metaphorical *identity arena* where voices, captions, lyrics, slogans, and websites constantly wave their proverbial arms to get our attention and tell us who we are--or who we should be and what we should be consuming. Just as we would sink in the middle of the ocean if we did not kick our legs and move our arms, we will sink in a sea of impressions—voices, words, images—if we are not deliberate about cultivating our identities in Christ and operating out of that identity alone.

Second, and more pressing, we are not blank slates upon which a personality, character trait, or attitude can be hard-wired into us. If the wind blows in the direction of multiple identities and a divided self, then *sin* is the sail tied to our backs that catches an opposing and stiff wind. This truth is power-fully illustrated in a short poem by William Blake. It reads:

> *This life's dim window of the soul,*
> *Distorts the Heavens from pole to pole,*
> *And goads you to believe a lie,*
> *When you see with, and not through the eye.*

Blake is giving attention to how we view the world. He begins with the conception that our eyes are not neutral screens on which to interpret the world, but rather they are "dim windows of the soul." Moreover, this hazy vision will lead us to see the world in a distorted way unless we see *through* the windows with a heart, a mind, and a conscience—a worldview that is whole and thus holy. Christians are invited to see themselves as persons who can see through the single eye of a biblical mind, an active heart, and moral reasoning and action that is Spirit-filled and congruent with the faith tradition. Otherwise, we will be deceived and fall prey to the lies all about us. Thankfully, we can remind ourselves of Jesus' words: "With man this is impossible, but with God all things are possible" (Matt. 19:26). Not only has God justified us through Christ's atoning sacrifice, but God has restored our power and capability to love and worship God, serve our neighbors, and live a whole and consistent life.

Conceiving of Work *as* Worship can free us as people of faith to view our labor activity—whatever field it may be in—as a worshipful activity. However, the key to this is not just changing the mind; it is living in God's fullness, being holy as God is and provides.

English writer G. K. Chesterton offers a fitting expression of this important concept. His 1905 essay "A Piece of Chalk" describes—in all of Chesterton's wit and wonder—the beauty and moral reality of white chalk. "White," he writes, "is a colour. It is not a mere absence of colour; it is a shining and affirmative thing, as fierce as red, as definite as black."[6] In other words, most assume that the color white is neutral: it is devoid of shade, absent of expression, and ultimately "non-committal." However, Chesterton asserts that white is not the absence of color, but rather the fullness of color—expressive, vibrant, positive, and demonstrative.

Likewise, virtue is not merely the absence of vices or the avoidance of moral dangers; virtue is a vivid and separate thing. Indeed, beyond a description of chalk, Chesterton provides us with a lucid picture of holiness. He says that it is not merely the absence of obvious sin, but the fullness and presence of God. Living whole is living with Spirit-filled integrity.

The full presence of God may be the key to a holy life, but it is equally part and parcel of a whole life. Being whole does not divorce our identities in an inappropriate way. Wholeness does not attempt to dance and fight. It does not "limp." It does not separate our faith life from other important aspects of our life. It recognizes that everything we think, say, and do can be an act of worship. This is *holiness*; this is *wholeness*. Being whole is not the absence of sin, pain, or vice; it is the full presence of God. Moreover, this presence crowds out space for other allegiances. It reveals and reflects a life that displays a unified, constant, and consistent act of worship as its central characteristic.

A Personal Example

The authors do not claim to have figured this all out. It is a life-long journey. As an aged and wise friend recently said, "I am glad that God is not finished with me…that would suggest that he has no more use for me." Well, we are not finished. We are two people who have both worked in a secular business setting and then found our ways into an academic life. The truth is, we have experienced the divides ourselves and still see elements of them in our own lives.

This book is really the product of personal experience, success and failure, along with sharing with a lot of other "workers" who feel that their lives are a bit schizophrenic and want to live a more whole life as Christians. Recently, this material was taught to a Sunday school class and the experience affirmed that this is a common issue that many Christians wrestle with. Another discovery is that other Christians are initially not bothered because they have found a way to live with one or more of the divides. It is interesting to see the change of mind when they consider whether Work *as* Worship should be an alternative.

There is a "fork in the road" point in each of our individual lives when we have to define how we approach work. As committed Christians, we want to live a life pleasing to God and in the model of Jesus. But, for us as young business persons in a secular world, we found ourselves in the Identity Arena and living the divides. Let us share how the transition occurred.

As young and aspiring business persons who were also Christians, our first tendency was to accept the Work *not* Worship divide as the necessary norm. When at church or at home, there was one standard, but the situation dictated another way at work, especially if we wanted to get ahead. That led to compromise and conflict between the holiness stance heard on Sunday and weekly practice. Knowing that this contrast was not right, we began to spiritualize everything, even our business enterprises. If we started a business and called it by a Christian name or used Christian talk when at work, then we thought of ourselves as okay.

In hindsight, it may have been the response to others in our church who questioned whether or not we could really be Christians if we were involved in marketing (the Work *or* Worship divide). The truth is that we were living two divides at the same time. For secular friends at work, we were "the Christians" who were not really that different from co-workers (other than that we did not swear or drink alcohol). Among our church friends, we were perceived as brash about how God was using us as business persons and falsely spiritualizing our plans to use business to make our marks. Is this the whole life?

For us, a change occurred over time through the example of influential mentors, teaching from books such as *Small is Beautiful: Economics as if People Matter*, and Lord *Change Me* in addition to Scripture. Specifically, biblical verses that changed our perspective included Colossians 3:23-24 and Romans 12:2. We realized that our focus was on working for the company or for our own success, and that this was misplaced. Instead, we needed to work "as unto the Lord."

One of us worked in a grocery store and then at a Christian college and realized that I wanted to allow God to "renew my mind." This realization impacted the way I engaged with others. The idea of "community" was the first change for me. Instead of seeing my co-workers at the grocery store as "sinners" or as "win-able." I allowed them to become my friends—good friends. That work setting became a healthy work community for me, and that was a dramatic change.

As the desire to worship God through work grew, there was a desire to be creative. Much of this time I was also a college student and what I was learning in class found applications at work. My boss at the store was very excited to let me try new things, even though this was not the corporate way. That led me to experiment with merchandising, signage, and even my work hours (I decided to work all night to make sure the department was ready for sales first thing in the morning). As I tried new things and had some success, I was encouraged by my boss to think bigger and bolder about my future and that led to opportunities that I enjoy today.

While at that time I did not think of it as being a "co-creator with God," I did understand that my new attitude about work resulted in a desire to let my work be a creative expression of the best that I was. As such, God was using my giftedness as a catalyst for his work. In the end, I left that job knowing that I had grown and that I had made a contribution.

The lessons as a young professional have followed me through the years. Now I find myself as a teacher who knows that my work is co-creating with God, a catalyst using my gifts to serve as a steward, and a way to build community and positive relationships. Finally, I have made a contribution to the lives of others, to the betterment of society, and to God's kingdom. What is most fulfilling now are the stories of students in the business world that have discovered that their work has meaning and purpose. No, not everything is perfect and we (the authors) are not perfect. Situations can be less then desirable and things do not always work out. Regardless, work is an act of worship. Work has made Jesus' admonition to be "salt and light" real in our lives. Good work honors God and as such it is worship.

Living Whole: Work *as* Worship

We want the fullness of God. Further, living within that fullness, we want all of our activity to be brought to the altar before God in an act of worship—including our work. We have suggested that work and worship should not be divided, nor should they be inappropriately married. Rather, we begin with our faith identity, and then see, understand, and act in and for the world based upon that identity. *We see through the eyes of our faith identity.*

Christians must become equipped to view, process, and act upon a world in a faithful way. In addition to "taking every thought captive and making it obedient to Christ" (2 Cor. 10:5), activity is "salt and light" so as to "honor and glorify the Lord" (Matt. 5:16). Our identity as a Christian, cultivated and refined through the faith community, is our lens by which to perceive and engage the world around us.

Perceive your work not as something else you do in your life disconnected from your faith, but as an act of worship. Live out the 4 C's: *Co-Creating* with your Creator, being a *Catalyst* for God's kingdom with your gifts, creating *Community* through your activity, and making a lasting and faithful *Contribution* to the world around you. Finally, understand that your strength, your identity, and your wholeness is not determined so much by the absence of sin and alternate identities in your life, but rather by the fullness of God at the center of your life.

It is time to go to work. Go! Go to work and worship. Find wholeness and holiness as you express your love for God through your work activities.

ENDNOTES

1 Clark M. Williamson and Ronald J. Allen, *Adventures of the Spirit: A Guide to Worship from the Perspective of Process Theology* (Lanham: University of America, 1997), 70.

2 Michael J. Sandel, *What Money Can't Buy: The Moral Limits of Markets* (New York: Farrar, Straus and Giroux, 2012), 200.

3 Pallab Ghosh, "Web 'Re-defining' Human Identity Says Chief Scientist." BBC News. BBC, 21 Jan. 2013. Web. 25 Apr. 2013.

4 Lee C. Camp, *Mere Discipleship: Radical Christianity in a Rebellious World* (Grand Rapids: Brazos, 2003), 181.

5 A. W. Tozer, *The Knowledge of the Holy: The Attributes of God, Their Meaning in the Christian Life* (New York: Harper & Row, 1961), 7.

6 G. K. Chesterton, "A Piece of Chalk," in A Piece of Chalk. N.p., n.d. Web. 07 May 2013.

Lightning Source UK Ltd.
Milton Keynes UK
UKHW021955030120
356334UK00007B/1697/P